Biblical Themes

Biblical Themes

A Thematic Summary of Biblical Theology

John P. Davis

Foreword by Craig Biehl

WIPF & STOCK · Eugene, Oregon

BIBLICAL THEMES
A Thematic Summary of Biblical Theology

Wipf & Stock
An Imprint of Wipf and Stock Publishers
199 W. 8th Ave., Suite 3
Eugene, OR 97401

www.wipfandstock.com

PAPERBACK ISBN: 978-1-6667-3739-4
HARDCOVER ISBN: 978-1-6667-9676-6
EBOOK ISBN: 978-1-6667-9677-3

MARCH 25, 2022 9:33 AM

Contents

Foreword

Dr. Craig Biehl

God created all things. From the immeasurable grandeur of the heavens to the smallest particles on earth, the universe and everything in it declare the power and genius of God. Together they form the stage on which God performs His greatest work. From the overflow of His goodness, God made Adam and Eve. He gave them every good to enjoy in paradise, including the immeasurable privilege of loving communion with the sovereign and benevolent Lord of the universe. Moreover, by the smallest display of fidelity He would give them access to the Tree of Life, that Adam and his posterity might enjoy holiness and happiness—forever—as blessed children of God.

But they fell. In a bold act of rebellion and ingratitude, they chose their own will and the word of a lying serpent over the authority and will of their loving Maker and Sustainer. They sinned and treated with contempt the One to whom they owed all love, honor, and obedience. Adam, in particular, brought God's curse upon himself, Eve, and mankind, including the confirmed inclination behind his disastrous choice. As threatened by God, Adam and Eve died spiritually when they partook of the forbidden fruit, while their physical death would come in due time.

And mankind died with them. As Adam stood as our representative in his easy trial of obedience, he lost paradise for everyone. His descendants now enter a fallen and cursed world under the just judgment of God, possessed of the very inclination by which Adam chose death over true life. And never again would God offer eternal life by our obedience. Our best efforts, tears, or good works could never regain a right relationship with God. Our highest acts of virtue became as filthy rags to a holy God, even as our loving Father became our enemy and judge.

We were helpless and hopeless. God's justice required our punishment while it forbade the pardon of a single soul. God cannot extend His mercy without the satisfaction of His justice, a justice requiring spiritual and eternal death for sin. Thus, to save the unsavable, God would need to perform a greater work than the creation of heaven and earth. An infinite debt would need to be paid, though no creature on earth or angel in heaven could pay it. How, then, would the lost be saved? How would rebels with hearts of stone gain hearts of love to God? And how would the justice and infinite excellence of God be vindicated?

God has told us. From the first words of Genesis to the closing words of the Book of Revelation, we see the glory of God in the design and accomplishment of our redemption. The opening chapters begin God's foreshadowing and explanation of His purpose and plan of the ages. In His curse upon Adam, Eve, and the serpent, we see a glimmer of God's glory in our deliverance by the seed of the woman crushing the serpent's head. And as God's revelation gradually unfolds His eternal plan through His words and acts in history, recorded in Scripture by the Holy Spirit through the prophets and Apostles, the various themes progressively merge to form a beautiful picture of God's infinite excellence—most clearly displayed in the person and work of Christ to rescue His beloved but lost bride.

In this helpful and handy booklet, John Davis provides a succinct outline and summary of the themes of Scripture that form for us that final and glorious picture of God's purpose of the ages. Drawing from Scripture and the works of several scholars expounding what theologians call *biblical theology*, John introduces the nature and purpose of various biblical themes. He provides us with a helpful and memorable framework of the biblical themes of Christ, Creation, Corruption, Covenant, Church, and Consummation.

For those new to *biblical theology*, as distinguished from *systematic theology*, or for those who have yet to plumb the depths of more comprehensive works on the topic, you will appreciate this concise introduction, outline, and summary of the marvelous themes of Scripture that point us to Christ. You will be blessed at seeing the unified and consistent nature of Scripture as it reflects the coherent mind of its Author, and the marvelous way that God has woven multi-colored threads to form a beautiful tapestry of God's infinite excellence, an excellence most clearly seen in the person and work of Christ in His redemption of sinners. May the truths presented here lead to praise of the great God that has chosen the sinful and unworthy to be the bride of Christ, to be holy and happy in heaven, forever, as trophies of His grace.

Introduction

As a young, nineteen-year-old new believer in 1970, I had an insatiable appetite to understand the Bible. Fifty-one years later that hunger persists. I do not think I really understood biblical theology in the sense set forth by Geerhardus Vos[1] until my time at Westminster Theological Seminary beginning in 1986, especially in the course entitle *Old Testament Biblical Theology*, taught by Dr. Bruce Waltke. As a young Christian I had read Eric Sauer's *The Dawn of World Redemption*, as well as other dispensational books, which sought to provide a coherent and unified message to the Bible. I read most of what Walter C. Kaiser had written and appreciated his focus on promise as a unifying theme, and in seminary I was introduced to Geerhardus Vos's *Biblical Theology: Old and New Testaments*, which ignited a deeper desire for the theology of the Bible. These samplings of biblical theology were engaging but remained peripheral in my study of the Bible, until my time at Westminster. At Westminster my eyes were opened wonderfully to the glory of Jesus Christ in all of Scripture.

The Triune God has given us the sixty-six books of Scripture to point us to the sufficiency of the person and work of Jesus Christ. Through that perfect redemptive work of Jesus, as recorded in Scripture, both sinners and the cosmos are restored from the

---

1. "Biblical Theology, rightly defined, is nothing else than the exhibition of the organic progress of supernatural revelation in its historic continuity and multiformity" (Vos, *Inauguration*, 1894).

ruinous effects of the fall. I experienced that redemption and began a process of restoration in 1970.

Jesus is the central theme of Scripture. All secondary themes find their meaning and significance in their relationship to His person and work. In this summary of biblical themes, we will see how the themes of Creation, Corruption, Covenant, Church, and Consummation each are understood in relationship to Jesus Christ, and how, because of Jesus Christ, they each relate to each other.

God's final Word is spoken through Jesus Christ. Later in chapter three I will repeat some of what I say here about Christ being the final and fullest revelation from God. It is through the lens of that full and final revelation in Christ that we look at all of Scripture.

The words of Jesus Christ lead us to conclude that the OT is "progressive, redemptive revelation. It is revelation because in it God makes himself known. It is redemptive because God reveals himself in the act of redeeming us. It is progressive because God makes himself and his purposes known by stages until the full light is revealed in Jesus Christ."[2]

This progressive, redemptive revelation of Jesus Christ is given through historical events, people, promises, institutions, Christophanies, etc., all of which in some way anticipate or foreshadow the final and full revelation in Jesus Christ.

Goldsworthy sums up the relationship of Jesus Christ to the OT:

> The New Testament emphasizes the historic person of Christ and what he did for us, through faith, to become the friends of God. The emphasis is also on him as the one who sums up and brings to their fitting climax all the promises and expectations raised in the Old Testament. There is a priority of order here, which we must take into account if we are to understand the Bible correctly. It is the gospel event, as that which brings about faith

2. Goldsworthy, *According to Plan*, 72. Like slowly turning on the dimmer in your dining room as images move from darkness to outlines of objects, to shadows, to clear sight.

in the people of God, that will motivate, direct, pattern, and empower the life of the Christian community. So we start from the gospel and move to an understanding of Christian living, and the final goal toward which we are moving.

Again, we start from the gospel and move back into the Old Testament to see what lies behind the person and work of Christ. The Old Testament is not completely superseded by the gospel, for that would make it irrelevant to us. It helps us understand the gospel by showing us the origins and meanings of the various ideas and special words used to describe Christ and his works in the New Testament. Yet we must also recognize that Christ is God's fullest and final Word to mankind. As such he reveals to us the final meaning of the Old Testament.[3]

I hope that my summary of biblical themes will assist and encourage your journey in understanding and enjoying the Bible. Most importantly, I pray that the Spirit of God through the Word of God will enable you to see more of the superior glory of Jesus Christ.

---

3. Goldsworthy, *According to Plan*, 106–7.

CHAPTER ONE

Introduction to Biblical Themes
(Part One)

What are Biblical Themes?

BIBLICAL THEMES are those primary, theologically rich ideas of Scripture introduced early in seed form and developed progressively in the history of revelation. The discovery of these themes is arrived at through the discipline of Biblical Theology.

That raises the question: What is Biblical Theology? Here we will accept Geerhardus Vos's definition as contained in his inaugural address at Princeton Seminary in 1894. "Biblical Theology, rightly defined, is nothing else than the exhibition of the organic progress of supernatural revelation in its historic continuity and multiformity."[1]

What does the study of Biblical Theology involve? The following Theses[2] explain the approach to studying Scripture called "Biblical Theology."

---

1. Vos, *Inauguration*, 1894.

2. Presented by Richard Schultz and Scott Hafemann at the ETS Annual Meeting in 1998 with the addition of Theses 3 by John P. Davis.

1. Biblical Theology should be biblical, taking the entire canon in its entirety as its starting point and criterion.

2. Biblical Theology should be theological, aiming at making synthetic assertions about the nature, will, and plan of God in creation and redemption, as well as their corresponding implications for the nature, will, and purpose of humanity.

3. Biblical Theology should be Christological, understanding that God's fullest and final revelation is in Jesus Christ, who then becomes the interpretive center of Scriptures.

4. Biblical Theology should be historical, contextual, and thematic in its methodology, integrating historical development, literary structures, socio-cultural factors, and theological concepts within an understanding of the history of redemption.

5. Biblical Theology should develop its theological categories inductively from the biblical text, not from a predetermined systematic framework.

6. Biblical Theology should be exegetically based, taking intertextuality as its starting point, including both the OT use of the OT and the NT use of the OT as preserved in the MT and LXX traditions.

7. Biblical Theology should be intentionally bi-testamental and unifying, so that neither the OT nor the NT are read in isolation from each other nor from the standpoint of a "canon within the canon."

8. Biblical Theology should work toward a unity of the canon, going beyond the traditional disciplines of OT and NT theology and beyond providing simply descriptive accounts of the various theological emphases within its individual writings.

9. Biblical Theology should strive to incorporate the diversity of the biblical writings within the unity of theology, without sacrificing either its historical particularity or its overarching history of redemption.

10. Biblical Theology should be both descriptive and prescriptive in order to be faithful to its theological task of providing an enduring contribution to the self-understanding of God's people within their contemporary context.

11. Biblical Theology should be pursued by means of an intentional dialogue within the body of Christ in order to overcome the lamentable specialization of biblical scholars and be viewed as a profoundly spiritual calling in order to be faithful to the biblical witness.

Why study Biblical Themes within a biblical-theological framework?

We desire to communicate and reinforce a biblical worldview that has the following characteristics:

1. a biblical worldview of which everyone is self-conscious;

2. a biblical worldview which is succinct, yet comprehensive;

3. a biblical worldview which is transferable on a church-wide level;

4. a biblical worldview which sees the individual portions of Scripture in relationship to the whole;

5. a biblical worldview which adequately serves as an apologetic for the gospel.

Understanding Biblical Themes within a biblical-theological approach will reinforce at least the following:

1. an ahistorical and universal explanation of the world and humanity;

2. an humble approach toward epistemological certainty grounded in God's revelation;

3. a spirituality that is rooted in objective revelation;

4. a message of salvation that is exclusively based on faith in the death and resurrection of Jesus Christ;

5. an understanding of morality that views sin as offense against the God Who is there;

6. a subordination of personal experience to objective truth;

7. a passion to share all of the above with a lost and dying world.

Many have attempted to find a single-unifying theme around which to gather all of Biblical Theology.[3] Gerhard Hasel has adequately shown the shortfalls of these attempts in his discussion on Old Testament Biblical Theology:

> Since no single theme or, scheme, or motif is sufficiently comprehensive to include within it all the varieties of OT viewpoints, one must refrain from using a particular concept, formula, basic idea, etc., as the center of the OT whereby a systematization of the manifold and variegated OT testimonies is achieved.[4]

What Hasel says may be applied to New Testament Biblical Theology as well as biblical theology in general.

The Relationship of Systematic Theology to Biblical Theology

It is important to not discount the contributions of systematic theology, but rather to view them and teach them in their relationship to Biblical Theology.

Relationship of Systematic Theology to Biblical Theology

Creation	Corruption	Covenant	Christ	Church	Consummation
Revelation	>>>>>	>>>>>	>>>>>	>>>>>	>>>>>
God	>>>>>	>>>>>	>>>>>	>>>>>	>>>>>
Man	>>>>>	>>>>>	>>>>>	>>>>>	>>>>>

3. For instance: a thematic center (Eichrodt, Kaiser); a confessional center (Eissfeldt); a kerygmatic tradition (von Rad); categories of God, man, salvation (various); from a vantage point of the New Testament (Childs); around an exegetical center (Martens). (Waltke, *Old Testament Biblical Theology*, 8).

4. Hasel, *Old Testament Theology*, 179.

Sin	>>>>>	>>>>>	>>>>>	>>>>>	>>>>>
Christ	>>>>>	>>>>>	>>>>>	>>>>>	>>>>>
Spirit	>>>>>	>>>>>	>>>>>	>>>>>	>>>>>
Salvation	>>>>>	>>>>>	>>>>>	>>>>>	>>>>>
Church	>>>>>	>>>>>	>>>>>	>>>>>	>>>>>
Last Things	>>>>>	>>>>>	>>>>>	>>>>>	>>>>>

Geerhardus Vos has aptly summarized this approach saying,

> There is no better safeguard against that one-sidedness in the appreciation of truth, which is the source of all heresy, than an intelligent insight into the vital, organic, relation which any one doctrine sustains to all others . . . in its original historic setting. . . . that system will hold the field which can show that its doctrines grow organically on the stem of revelation, and are interwoven with its whole structure from beginning to end.[5]

In this book I will set forth a biblical-theological approach built around six major biblical themes/events that comprise the essential story of the Bible. For the sake of memory, those themes/events are alliterated. They are 1) Creation, 2) Corruption, 3) Covenant[6,] 4) Christ, 5) Church, 6) Consummation.

These particular themes/events are selected for the following reasons:

1. they offer six pivotal perspectives of divine purpose;

2. they offer six streams of thought that lead us to Jesus Christ;

3. they focus on six critical movements on the plot line of re-demptive history;

4. they highlight six theological realities that we deny at our own peril

5. Vos in *Kerux*, May 1999, 7–8.

6. By "covenant" I mean a bond (or relationship) that God establishes with man by His speaking (His Words). Of primary interest is the role of the Abrahamic Covenant.

For the sake of utilizing a visual learning device, I suggest that these six themes/events be illustrated as follows:

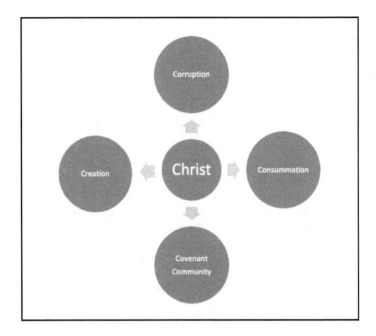

This illustration offers some helpful analogies for biblical-theological teaching.

Christ is at the center of Biblical Theology. All biblical themes are understood in relationship to Christ.

The Christ-centered movement from creation to consummation and from corruption to covenant and community is both a vertical and horizontal movement. It reminds uss that Biblical Theology is both chronological and eschatological. By "eschatology" I mean what Geerhardus Vos meant when he spoke of those points in history where God (the heavenly/eschatological) decisively penetrates the earthly order. God penetrates the order in His acts but primarily does so through verbal revelation.

The central focus of Biblical Theology is Jesus Christ and His work of redemption accomplished at the Cross. Christ is the centerpiece of God's plan for redeeming a fallen world. Christ is at the center of creation and consummation. Christ is also at the center of

God's covenant relationship with His people and His church into which His people are gathered. Christ is at the heart of both the chronological and eschatological aspects of Biblical Theology. The central position of Christ reminds us that God's relationship both with the movement of history (Creation to Consummation) and with the His redemption of mankind (Corruption to Covenant to Community is centered in Christ.

In each of these themes/events of Biblical Theology God and man are presented in varying relationships and the particular focus of the sphere of the rule of God/Christ is suggested, as follows:

Creation	*Corruption*	*Covenant*
Christ as Creator & Ruler Man as creature & sub-regent All = Christ's kingdom. (CK)	Christ as One rebelled against Man as rebel Satan's Kingdom/ Christ's kingdom	Christ as Covenant-Maker Man as covenant keeper/breaker Abraham's Seed = CK
Cross	*Church*	*Consummation*
Christ as Redeemer and Covenant Keeper/ Fulfiller Man as sinner & rebel Redeemed = CK	Christ as King Man as servant Church = CK	Christ as Judge Man as Covenant Keeper/Breaker All = CK

The rest of this book will be an amplification of the six biblical themes.

CHAPTER TWO

Introduction to Biblical Themes

(Part Two)

THIS CHAPTER touches on a few more introductory matters that lay a framework for our study of biblical themes. Biblical themes, as we have seen, are derived from an approach to the Bible called biblical theology. Again, we will start with the definition offered by Geerhardus Vos: "Biblical Theology, rightly defined, is nothing else than the "exhibition of the organic progress of supernatural revelation in its historic continuity and multiformity."[1]

The book by Graeme Goldsworthy suggests a number of benefits of having a biblical-theological approach.

1. Biblical Theology gives us the means to deal with problem passages of the Bible by relating them to the one message of the Bible.

2. Biblical Theology enables us to relate any Bible story to the whole message of the Bible, and, therefore, to ourselves.

3. Biblical Theology shows the relationship of all parts of the Old Testament to the person and work of Jesus Christ and, therefore, to the Christian.

---

1. Vos, *Inauguration.*

4. Biblical Theology enables us to map out the unity of the Bible by looking at its message as a whole.

5. Biblical Theology provides the basis for the interpretation of any part of the Bible as God's Word to us.[2]

Let me illustrate how Biblical Theology aids in responding to a life-situation. An English teacher in a local high school taught that the stories of Adam, Eve, Cain, and Abel are myth. I wrote to him and asked for equal time to present the view that the biblical record is history. I am aware that there are many archaeological and historical evidences that corroborate the OT narratives as history. But as a Christian, there's a more crucial point from Biblical Theology. When you consider the unity of the Bible, the relationship of the two testaments, the OT anticipation and foreshadowing of Christ, the NT fulfillment of the OT, then you understand that calling the OT narratives myth is a frontal attack on Christianity, whose founder, Jesus Christ, affirmed their historicity. You don't come to that conclusion by reading Genesis, you come to it by the full and final revelation in Christ.

So, as you begin to think in a biblical-theological way, you start with Christ; you think about relationships between testaments; you think about the historical development of doctrine; you think about promise and fulfillment; you think about the how things fit into the big picture; you think about how they all are tied together; you think about the beginning and the end and where you fit at this moment in the plan of God.

Knowing God and being known by Him

Biblical Theology is an approach to Scripture that assists us in becoming better theologians. As Goldsworthy points out, "Every Christian by definition knows God, thinks about God, and makes statements about God. So, you are a theologian."[3]

---

2. Goldsworthy, *According to Plan*, 24–29.
3. Goldsworthy, *According to Plan*, 34.

As a believer you have the privilege of knowing God through His Word - acquiring and systematizing that knowledge. Previously, we briefly looked at how different approaches to theology compare.

For a moment let's compare them so we can better understand Biblical Theology.[4]

- Systematic Theology asks the question: What should Christians believe now about any aspect of Christianity?

- Historical Theology asks the question: What have Christians believed about their faith at any given time?

- Exegetical Theology asks the question: What is the intentional meaning of a particular text?

- Practical Theology asks the question: How does the Word of God apply to my life so that I may mature in Christian living?

- Biblical Theology asks the question: By what process has God revealed Himself to mankind?

For an accurate knowledge of God, we are dependent upon God's self-revelation.

Revelation implies a difference between God's knowledge and man's knowledge. Let me explain by asking and answering a few questions regarding knowledge:

1. What does God know? His knowledge is comprehensive and self-contained. (God never learned anything.)

2. How does God reveal what He knows? God's revelation is both natural and special. Natural revelation is the disclosure of His power and glory in the created universe. Special revelation is the disclosure of His redemptive purposes through Scripture. In the past special revelation included appearances of God and the incarnation of Jesus Christ.

4. Goldsworthy, *According to Plan*, 34–41.

3. What do men, as creatures, know? Generally, all of their knowledge is limited and derived. They are dependent upon God for knowledge.

4. What can a lost man know?

   a. He can know some things accurately from natural revelation;

   b. He can know nothing completely – he lacks an integrated view that relates all to Christ;

   c. He cannot comprehend some things (special revelation) at all. He doesn't know God.

5. What can a saved man know? He has free access to all of God's revelation, both natural and special.

6. How does a saved man know? Through the two eyes of faith and reason he looks into the room of knowledge. The Spirit of God turns the light on in the room. Through the single lens of revelation of Jesus Christ everything is brought into proper focus. A lost man has only the single eye of reason, but even that is out of focus, and he peers into a dark room.

There are actually three views of how one can know the truth.[5]

The first view (Secular Humanism) supposes that man is totally independent of a God who either does not exist or who is irrelevant. Man is in control of knowledge that he acquires through his senses and reason. In this view the Bible is just another book without any supernatural character.

The second view (Theistic Humanism) holds that man is only partly independent of God. Man by reason can know the world in which he lives. He depends upon revelation for "religious" knowledge that is added to what he already knows. Francis Schaeffer called this a two-story view where faith and reason never intersect.

5. Goldsworthy, *According to Plan*, 45–56.

This view has a very weak view of the fall and how the fall has affected man's thinking. Often in this view human reason stands in judgment on the Bible and decides which revelation to accept or reject.

The third view (Christian Theism) holds that all knowledge is dependent upon God. Since God is Creator of all, all facts are somehow related to God and dependent upon Him for interpretation. This view recognizes that the fall causes all men to suppress the truth and that without regeneration men can never know the truth about God and men will never see any truth in its proper relationship to God.

Goldsworthy offers us five presuppositions that are the underpinnings of our study of biblical themes:

1. God made every fact in the universe and He alone can interpret all things and events.

2. Because we are created in the image of God, we know that we are dependent upon God for the truth.

3. As sinners we suppress this knowledge and reinterpret the universe on the assumption that we, not God, give things their meaning.

4. Special revelation through God's redemptive word, reaching its high point in Jesus Christ, is needed to deal with our suppression of the truth and hostility to God.

5. A special work of the Holy Spirit brings repentance and faith so that sinners acknowledge the truth which is in Scripture.[6]

---

6. Goldsworthy, *According to Plan*, 56.

CHAPTER THREE

The Biblical Theme of Christ

Read: pages 58–114 in Goldsworthy, *According to Plan.*

JESUS IS the eternal Son of God, the second Adam, the Creator of the world, the One who suffers the curse of the law for us, the sinless covenant-keeper, the quintessential seed of Abraham, heir to the Davidic throne, the Messiah, the Lord of the Church, and the final Judge of the world. He gave His life in payment for sin to redeem sinners and to restore them to God's original and eternal purposes. In so doing, He sets in motion the regaining of all that was lost in the fall.

Goldsworthy points out that "the one problem we have in the interpretation of the Bible is the failure to interpret the texts by the definitive event of the gospel."[1] Jesus Christ, as the final and fullest revelation of God, is the key to understanding both Old and New Testaments.

The incarnation of Jesus Christ signaled that the age of fulfillment had arrived.

Each of the gospel writers is careful to connect Jesus Christ to the Old Testament. Throughout Matthew we find "fulfilled" eighteen times (1:1–17, 21; 1:22; 2:15; 2:17; 2:23; 3:15; 4:14; 5:17; 8:17; 12:17; 13:35; 13:48; 21:4; 23:32; 26:54; 26:56; 27:9). We also find "It was written" ten times (2:5; 4:4; 4:6; 4:7; 4:10; 11:10; 21:13; 26:24;

1. Goldsworthy, *According to Plan*, 62.

13

26:31; 27:37). Additionally, we find "Spoken through the prophet" four times (1:22; 2:15; 2:17; 4:14). Mark introduces his gospel with an OT connection in 1:1–3. In the birth narratives Luke speaks of the OT connection to Zechariah, Mary, Angels to Shepherds, Simeon, and Anna. Luke also offers a genealogy that takes Christ back through Israel to Adam, and then to God. In Luke 24 the gospel writer records Jesus' affirming that the Old Testament anticipated him (24:25–27; 44–7). The Gospel of John makes numerous Old Testament connections in identifying Jesus as the Lamb of God, Bread of Life, the "I AM", etc. The epistles affirm in many ways the connection between Christ and the Old Testament.

For instance, look at these texts from 1 Corinthians and Hebrews.

> 1 Cor 10:1 For I do not want you to be ignorant of the fact, brothers, that our forefathers were all under the cloud and that they all passed through the sea. 2 They were all baptized into Moses in the cloud and in the sea. 3 They all ate the same spiritual food 4 and drank the same spiritual drink; for they drank from the spiritual rock that accompanied them, and that rock was Christ. 5 Nevertheless, God was not pleased with most of them; their bodies were scattered over the desert. 6 Now these things occurred as examples to keep us from setting our hearts on evil things as they did. 7 Do not be idolaters, as some of them were; as it is written: "The people sat down to eat and drink and got up to indulge in pagan revelry." 8 We should not commit sexual immorality, as some of them did-- and in one day twenty-three thousands of them died. 9 We should not test the Lord, as some of them did-- and were killed by snakes. 10 And do not grumble, as some of them did-- and were killed by the destroying angel. 11 These things happened to them as examples and were written down as warnings for us, on whom the fulfillment of the ages has come.

> Heb 8: 5 They serve at a sanctuary that is a copy and shadow of what is in heaven. This is why Moses was

warned when he was about to build the tabernacle: "See to it that you make everything according to the pattern shown you on the mountain."

Heb 10:1 The law is only a shadow of the good things that are coming-- not the realities themselves. For this reason, the same sacrifices repeated endlessly year after year could never make perfect those who draw near to worship.

Hebrews 8 declares that the Old Covenant is obsolete with the arrival of New Covenant.

Old Covenant Shadows	New Covenant Realities
Mosaic Law	Law of Christ
Temple	Christ and His Church
Animal Sacrifice	Sacrifice of Christ
Aaronic Priesthood	Priesthood of Christ
Old Covenant	New Covenant
Monarchy	Christ as King
Promised Land	Rest in Christ/Eternal Kingdom

Furthermore, Samuel Waldron notes that, because of the fulfillment in Christ, a comparison of the characteristics and privileges granted to Israel in the Old Testament are assumed by the church in the New Testament.[2]

Old Israel or the Church	New Israel or the Church
1. Saints (Num 16:3; Dt 33.3)	1. Saints (Eph 1:1; Rom 1:7)
2. Elect (Deut 7:6, 7; 14:2)	2. Elect (Col 3:12; Titus 1:1)
3. Beloved (Deut 7:7; 4:37)	3. Beloved (Col 3:12; 1 Thess 1:4)
4. Called (Isa 41:9; 43:1)	4. Called (Rom 1:6, 7; 1 Cor 1:2)
5. Church (Ps 89:5; Mic 2:5 (LXX)	5. Church (Eph 1:1; Acts 20:28; Acts 7:38; Heb 2:12)

2. Waldron, *End Times*, 143.

6. Flock (Ezek 34; Ps 77:20)	6. Flock (Luke 12:32; 1 Pet 5:2)
7. Holy Nation (Exod 19:5, 6)	7. Holy Nation (1 Pet 2:9)
8. Kingdom of Priests (Exod 19:5, 6)	8. Kingdom of Priests (1 Pet 2:9)
9. Peculiar Treasure (Exod 19:5, 6)	9. Peculiar Treasure (1 Pet 2:9)
10. God's People (Hos 1:9, 10)	10. God's People (1 Pet 2:10)
11. Holy People (Deut 7:6)	11. Holy People (1 Pet 1:15–16)
12. People of Inheritance (Deut 4:20)	12. People of Inheritance (Eph 1:18)
13. God's Tabernacle in Israel (Lev 26:11)	13. God's Tabernacle in Church (John 1:14)
14. God walks among them (Lev 26:12)	14. God walks among them (2 Cor 6:16–18)
15. Twelve Patriarchs	15. Twelve Apostles
16. Christ married to them (Jer 3:13; Hos 2:19; Jer 6:2; 31:32)	16. Christ married to them (Eph 5:22, 23; 2 Cor 11:12)

The Incarnation of Jesus Christ

When we study theology, i.e., the doctrine of God, we face a tension between two truths:

1. God is beyond and above the world. He is self-sufficient apart from the world;

2. God is present in the world. He is active in the processes of the universe and human history.

Imbalance on either of these truths leads to serious theological problems. Two extremes that illustrate this danger are deism and pantheism. Deism believes that God created the world but takes no further part in its functioning. On the other hand, pantheism believes that all laws, forces, and manifestations of the self-existing universe are god. God is not independent from the world.

Deism neglects that truth that God is present in the world. Pantheism neglects the truth that God is above and beyond the world. In both extremes God is useless--if He is present but not above the world, He cannot help; if He is not above the world though present, He cannot help.

Practically, when you over emphasize the truth that God is beyond the world, you face the danger of being irrelevant to the culture in which you live. If you over emphasize the truth that God is present in the world you produce a theology that becomes captive to a particular culture.

The incarnation of Jesus Christ brings together these two truths: He remains the God who is above and beyond the world; yet at the same time, He is present and active in the world. In His incarnation, He tells the world that He is relevant to every culture. John 1:1–18 sets forth the uniqueness of Jesus Christ. This text affirms both his "transcendence" and his "immanence."

Let us look briefly at some things this text teaches us about:

The Person of the Incarnation (His transcendence)

What do we learn here about Jesus - the God of the Incarnation?

The Word was in the beginning - speaking here of the absolute beginning of time. Compare to Genesis 1:1. In John 17 Jesus asks the Father to restore to Him the glory that he had before the world was. "The Word" emphasizes that Jesus is the Message of God. The Greek philosopher Philo has spoken of the LOGOS (Greek for "word") as a non-personal power of God creatively at work in the world. John affirms that LOGOS is a person, having the nature of God Himself.

The Word was with God (*pros ton theon*, speaking of His presence with the Father) Literally, "to the God", a phrase which is used 20 times in the Greek NT. A preposition of direction, i.e., "toward". We pray to God (Acts 12:5; Rom.10:1); we have peace with God (Rom 5:1); men blaspheme toward God (Rev 13:6); conversion is described as turning to God (1 Thess 1:9); faith is directed to God (1 Thess 1:8). Prior to creation, there was the Triune God and only the Triune God. Jesus was with God. He was present with God. He was occupied with God. He was in relationship with God. He was focused on God. All there was, was God.

Our text continues. Not only was he with God, *He was God.* In the beginning He was with God because He was God. Only God was in the beginning. If Jesus were not God, then he could not be in the beginning.

The Word was God (The absence of the Greek definite article speaks of His essence, His being) Contrary to the New World Translation of the JW's, there is no indefinite article in the Greek text, i.e., not "a god" but "God." When a noun is used without the article with an equative ("to be") verb, the idea normally is one of describing the character or quality of something or someone. In the Greek text the emphasis is on the word "God". It literally reads: "And God was the Word," i.e., the Word has the same quality of being as God does.

Remember the words of Thomas as he placed his fingers in the side of the risen Christ, "My Lord and my God" (John 21:29). Or the words of Paul as he speaks of Jesus "He is over all, God blessed forever" (Rom 9:5). Or the words of Jesus himself, "I and my Father are one" (John 10:30).

"This one was in the beginning with God."

1. He created all things - He is Lord of all creation - to receive the impact of verse 14, we must appreciate the truth of this verse. Who is this one who took on human flesh? The very one who created human flesh. Who is this one who enters this world of time, space, and matter? The very one who created time, space, and matter.

2. He is the source of life, bringing light to the world.

One of the great themes of John is that Jesus is life and that all light (spiritual illumination) comes from Jesus. Men can only have light to know God through Jesus Christ.

The Plan of the Incarnation (His immanence)
v. 14 - "the Word became flesh . . . "

In the incarnation the Son of God acquired a human form and a human nature without change in His divine nature and personality. Jesus remained one person with two natures. Just as there is a mystery in understanding the Trinity, there is a mystery in understanding that Jesus is both Perfect God and Perfect Man.

The fact that He became flesh means that the Son of God took on a corporeal, material, tangible, and visible form of humanity, identifying with us in our humanness, not our sinfulness.

In becoming flesh, He marks the beginning of fulfillment of the Old Testament promise. He is Son of Man, son of Abraham, son of David, an Israelite, a prophet, priest, and king.

The Purpose of the Incarnation

What does it mean that Jesus has come in the flesh? Our text answers that question in two ways:

Jesus reveals the glory of God.

In eternity past, the Holy Trinity experienced complete satisfaction in the glory that they shared together. The glory of God is the awesomeness of His character, the brilliance of His majesty, and the infinite perfections of His being. The glory they shared together as the Triune God was sufficient for them.

However, they delighted in creating the world and humankind so we can see the glory of God. It is this glimpse of the glory of God that brings satisfaction and sufficiency into our lives. Remember Moses' request that God would show him His glory. Somehow in all that is happening in your life, God wants you to see His glory. Whether it's through the manifold gifts that He may bring your way or whether it's through the pain and suffering that God has providentially brought to pass, God wants us to see His glory. You can only see the glory of God through Jesus Christ.

The Hebrew word for glory is the word for being heavy (in weight). To give glory to someone was to recognize the weight that they carried in the community. To give glory to God is to truly recognize His supreme weight, i.e., His importance. Sometimes, we can be blinded to that and give glory that He deserves to idols. He has no equals. Often, we suffer loss so that we can see the greater glory of God. To suffer loss and not see that glory is tragic.

What does it mean that Jesus came in the flesh? You can see the glory of God.

Jesus brings grace and truth.

Jesus brings grace. He is full of grace. He offers favor and blessing to the undeserving (v. 16). Jesus brings truth. He is the truth. He reveals truth. Jesus Christ is God's Word for these last days. The Old Testament anticipated and foreshadowed Him, while the NT offers us a full revelation of Him. The following texts remind us that the OT is the word of God about Jesus Christ.

> Luke 24:25-27
> 25 He said to them, "How foolish you are, and how slow of heart to believe all that the prophets have spoken! 26 Did not the Christ have to suffer these things and then enter his glory?" 27 And beginning with Moses and all the Prophets, he explained to them what was said in all the Scriptures concerning himself.

> Luke 24:44-47
> 44 He said to them, "This is what I told you while I was still with you: Everything must be fulfilled that is written about me in the Law of Moses, the Prophets and the Psalms." 45 Then he opened their minds so they could understand the Scriptures. 46 He told them, "This is what is written: The Christ will suffer and rise from the dead on the third day, 47 and repentance and forgiveness of sins will be preached in his name to all nations, beginning at Jerusalem.

John 5:39–40

> 39 You diligently study the Scriptures because you think that by them you possess eternal life. These are the Scriptures that testify about me, 40 yet you refuse to come to me to have life.

The words of Jesus Christ lead us to conclude that the OT is "progressive, redemptive revelation. It is revelation because in it God makes himself known. It is redemptive because God reveals himself in the act of redeeming us. It is progressive because God makes himself and his purposes known by stages until the full light is revealed in Jesus Christ."[3]

This progressive, redemptive revelation of Jesus Christ is given through historical events, people, promises, institutions, Christophanies, etc., all of which in some way anticipate or foreshadow the final and full revelation in Jesus Christ.

Goldsworthy sums up the relationship of Jesus Christ to the OT:

> The New Testament emphasizes the historic person of Christ and what he did for us, through faith, to become the friends of God. The emphasis is also on him as the one who sums up and brings to their fitting climax all the promises and expectations raised in the Old Testament. There is a priority of order here, which we must take into account if we are to understand the Bible correctly. It is the gospel event, as that which brings about faith in the people of God, that will motivate, direct, pattern, and empower the life of the Christian community. So we start from the gospel and move to an understanding of Christian living, and the final goal toward which we are moving.
>
> Again, we start from the gospel and move back into the Old Testament to see what lies behind the person and work of Christ. The Old Testament is not completely superseded by the gospel, for that would make it irrelevant to us. It helps us understand the gospel by showing us

3. Goldsworthy, *According to Plan*, 72. Like slowly turning on the dimmer in your dining room as images move from darkness to outlines of objects, to shadows, to clear sight.

the origins and meanings of the various ideas and special words used to describe Christ and his works in the New Testament. Yet we must also recognize that Christ is God's fullest and final Word to mankind. As such he reveals to us the final meaning of the Old Testament.[4]

There are many studies that show the relationship of Christ to the Old Testament. An older two-volume study by E.W. Hengstenberg, *Christology of the Old Testament*, was written in 1854. This is a scholarly and detailed study (1400 pages) of Old Testament texts showing the prefiguring and prophecy of Jesus Christ in the Old Testament. A more recent study (1991) by Vern Poythress of Westminster Seminary, *The Shadow of Christ in the Law of Moses*, details how Christ is prefigured in the Pentateuch (5 books of Moses). A look at some of his chapter titles shows how starting with Christ and moving back into the Old Testament gives us insight into a fuller meaning of Christ.

1. The Tabernacle of Moses: Prefiguring God's Presence through Christ

2. The Sacrifices: Prefiguring the Final Sacrifice of Christ

3. The Priests and the People: Prefiguring Christ's Relation to His People

4. General Principles for God's Dwelling with Human Beings: Prefiguring Union with Christ.

5. The Land of Palestine, the Promised Land: Prefiguring Christ's Renewal and Dominion over the Earth.

6. The Law and Its Order: Prefiguring the Righteousness of Christ

7. The Purpose of the Tabernacle, the Law, and the Promised Land: Pointing Forward to Christ

8. The Punishments and Penalties of the Law: Prefiguring the Destruction of Sin and Guilt Through Christ

4. Goldsworthy, *According to Plan*, 106–7.

9. False Worship, Holy War, and Penal Substitution: Prefiguring the Spiritual Warfare of Christ and His Church.[5]

> I hope it is clear by now that Jesus Christ is the key to both the Old and New Testaments. We conclude this section with the words of Goldsworthy:
>
>> In order to know how any given part of the Bible relates to us, we must answer two prior questions: how does the text in question relate to Christ, and how do we relate to Christ? Since Christ is the *truth*, God's final and fullest word to mankind, all other words of the Bible are given their final meaning in him. The same Christ gives us our meaning and defines the significance of our existence in terms of our relationship to him.[6]

5. Poythress, *Shadow of Christ*, vii–ix.

6. Goldsworthy, *According to Plan*, 91.

CHAPTER FOUR

The Biblical Theme of Creation

Read: pages 115–29 in Goldsworthy, *According to Plan.*

Key Texts: Genesis 1–2; Psalm 8; John 1:1–3;
Colossians 1:15–20; Hebrews 1:1–3; Revelation 4:11

GENESIS 1–2 present Yahweh (Jesus Christ) as the Creator-King and humans as vice-regents of the great king.[1] In these chapters, creation is in harmony while in chapters 3–11 creation is in alienation. The Bible begins (Gen 1–2) and ends (Rev 21–22) with creation accounts. In between is the story of redemption. "The movement from creation to restoration is one organic development whereby God works out his plan for the redemption of a new humanity from all the nations (Rev 5:9; 7:9).[2]

The two creation accounts[3] serve at least three purposes:

1. They provide a theocentric perspective on creation with an anthropocentric focus. Genesis 1:1–2:3 teaches us that God

---

1. Vangemeren, *Progress of Redemption*, 33.

2. Vangemeren, *Progress of Redemption*, 40.

3. "Genesis 1 portrays God as a *ruler*, by whose command the world comes into being. The second account portrays God as a *potter* who shapes the man from the dust of the ground...." (Vangemeren, *Progress of Redemption*, 42).

makes a home for man and Genesis 2:4–25 shows us that God makes man at home in the world.

2. They are placed in the canon to show the Israelites that Yahweh was Creator. Yahweh is the God who creates. Confessing God as Creator demands that every created thing be related to him. Yahweh is also the God who speaks, who by fiat (word) brings the world into being. He is also the God who rules. Creation is witness to the glory of the Great King. Creation is witness to the power of the Great King. Creation is witness to the wisdom of the Great King. Vangemeren summarizes the importance of confessing God as Creator:

> The credo "I believe in the Creator" signified for Israel the confessional position that the whole world was the handiwork of the great King. By his Word the world of creation came into being. A belief in the Creator-God challenges any power attributed to gods of any mythological conception. Such a belief renounces absolute loyalty to any being or institution other than the great King and evokes a response of love, adoration, and worship. The great King endowed the world and especially humankind with his glory, power, and wisdom, and love. The great King has made everything but he has chosen men and women to respond to his love.[4]

3. Finally, Genesis 1–2 is the preamble to the history of redemption. In these chapters the rule of God over the earth is based on the fact that all of creation depends on God for its existence as well as its continuance. The nature of God's rule is one of order and faithfulness. God's description of the creation as "good" or "very good" speaks of God's pleasure with what He had made. However, we may imply that, since only the Sabbath was consecrated, the created world itself awaited consecration. When sin entered the world, consecration was no longer just a possibility; it now became a necessity. In creation Jesus Christ the great Redeemer/Restorer is anticipated.

4. Vangemeren, *Progress of Redemption*, 58.

God in his infinite wisdom created the world with a goal – the new creation in His Son, Jesus Christ. The New Creation is not simply a return to the original creation. It is better. The original creation was good (suitable for its purpose as a place of communion for God and man), but it was not perfect because of the human factor of the possibility of sin. The new creation will be "perfect, holy, and characterized by the presence of God the Father and the Lord Jesus Christ (Rev. 21:22). It is a world without pain, sin, or the possibility of sin, a world of the redeemed, whose bodies have been transformed gloriously."[5] The redemptive work of Jesus Christ was "no accident nor was it suddenly necessary in order to correct the course of an unforeseeably fallen creation, but it was fully in view when God created the world. Creation is, therefore, the beginning, or the preamble, of the history of redemption."[6]

We study Old Testament theology within the parameters of God's stated purpose for man as recorded in Genesis 1:26–27. An examination of this purpose discloses a two-fold, yet united, design for all humankind.

Primarily, God intended for man to have relationship with Himself. The term used to describe this relationship is "Sonship." Secondly, God intended that man should be responsible to Him and responsible for His creation. This responsibility is termed "Stewardship." This "Sonship/Stewardship" motif provides an initial paradigm for the study of Old Testament Biblical Theology. This Sonship/Stewardship motif is what we call the Kingdom of God.

This unique relationship that God has with man is described by Goldsworthy:

> Although God commits himself to the whole of creation
> for its good order and preservation, humanity is the spe-
> cial focus of this care. Creation is there for our benefit.
> Humanity is the representative of the whole creation
> so that God deals with creation on the basis of how he
> deals with humans. Only man is addressed as the one

5. Vangemeren, *Progress of Redemption*, 64.
6. Vangemeren, *Progress of Redemption*, 64.

who knows God and who is created to live purposefully for God. When man falls because of sin the creation is made to fall with him. In order to restore the whole of creation, God works through his Son who becomes a man to restore man.[7]

In the original creation God established the pattern for the kingdom of God.

> The pattern of the kingdom of God is this: God establishes a perfect creation which he loves and over which he rules. The highest honor is given to mankind as the only part of creation made in God's image. The kingdom means that everything in creation relates perfectly, that is, as God intends it should, to everything else and to God himself.[8]

It is important to point out that this prototype of the kingdom of God "differs radically from other kinds of world kingdoms that arose after the fall. This distinctive form of kingdom we call theocracy."[9] Eden in a special way was a theocracy. God established his presence there and so doing made Eden a sanctuary. Meredith Kline notes the special relationship within a theocracy:

> In a theocracy the people of the realm as well as the land itself are specially consecrated to God. This special religious relationship is defined through covenants, divinely determined and instituted, in which God identifies with the kingdom-people, bestowing on them his name to be borne and confessed by them. Because the name of God is identified with the theocratic people and is at stake in their history, the covenants that govern this relationship contain guarantees of dominion and power and glory for the loyal theocratic community.[10]

However, when we get to Genesis 3, we see that the fall of man disoriented man from fulfilling God's design. The fall necessitates

7. Goldsworthy, *According to Plan*, 103.
8. Goldsworthy, *According to Plan*, 127.
9. Kline, *Kingdom Prologue*, 32.
10. Kline, *Kingdom Prologue*, 33.

an additional motif that runs parallel to the first and that, at times, overshadows the first. From the event of the fall, there emerges a "Redemptive\Restoration" motif that continues throughout the Scripture.

Within the parameters of God's original intent of Sonship\Stewardship, paralleled by and at times overshadowed by Redemptive\Restoration, a paradigm for Old Testament Theology is set forth.

We will see later that the function of covenant relates to this overarching motif. The covenant served to ensure that there would be a seed to carry forth the Sonship\Stewardship purpose of God. The covenant grows out of the Redemptive\Restoration motif.

It is the above theological basis and understanding of the unity of the purpose of God that supplies certain normative features for making theological interpretations. When applied to the future covenants, this paradigm relates those covenants to the original purpose of God and establishes a unity and continuity in that purpose. In regard to the Abrahamic covenant Dumbrell notes: "The call of that patriarch began a program of redemption which aimed at full and final restoration of man and his world."[11]

Genesis 1:26–27, Psalm 8, and Hebrews 2 provide a basis for understanding man's ultimate place in this world. Man was commissioned with formative activity in the world. That formative activity was to be a reflection of his relationship to God and of his loyalty within that relationship. When the fall occurred, man exchanged his loyalty to God for loyalty to Satan. As a result, he became disoriented from God's intended purpose and, consequently, in need of restoration.

In Hebrews 2 Jesus Christ is presented as the perfect man, who macrocosmically fulfills Genesis 1:26–27, and through whom redeemed man may microcosmically fulfill that purpose. The macrocosmic fulfillment waits for the age of the kingdom and eternity, while the microcosmic fulfillment takes place in every age by those who have relationship to God and exercise loyalty to Him.

---

11. Dumbrell, *Covenant and Creation*, 50.

The primacy of the Great Commission emphasizes the exigency of seeing men restored to God's original purpose.

When men experience redemption, they then have the potential to fulfill God's original purpose in a microcosmic manner, awaiting the return of Jesus Christ for the ultimate and perfect fulfillment.

In the Mosaic economy the nation of Israel served as a model of a microcosmic fulfillment of Genesis 1:26–27. In the present age the church of Jesus Christ serves as a similar model. However, since both models demand of the participants a form of human responsibility, both are then subject to imperfection. Only in that future age under the dominion of Jesus Christ will ideal and perfect fulfillment take place.

As the biblical theme of creation is progressively unfolded in Scripture, we see these streams of thought emphasized and developed:

1. God, the Redeemer, is the Creator;

2. God rules over His creation in accordance with His royal nature (glory, power, wisdom, and fidelity);

3. His creation itself reflects these royal attributes;

4. Human beings are uniquely endowed to mirror the royal attributes of the great King;

5. God, who created by His Word, maintains His relationship with individuals by the Word;

6. Although the original creation was good, it had to be consecrated and perfected; therefore,

7. Jesus Christ had to come to consecrate all things to God (Eph 1:9–10).[12]

---

12. Vangemeren, *Progress of Redemption*, 40.

CHAPTER FIVE

The Biblical Theme of Corruption

Read: pages 130–53 in Goldsworthy, *According to Plan*.

THE EFFECTS of the fall were devastating and pervasive for the human race. The Scriptures are unequivocal in saying "... that Adam and Eve's fall into sin was not just an isolated act of disobedience but an event of catastrophic significance for creation as a whole."[1]

It is important to understand the relationship of sin to creation, to Covenant, to the cross, to the church, and to the consummation. But, first we will look at the entrance of human sin into the created order.

The entrance of human sin into the created order

The Bible does not offer an explanation of how evil entered the universe. We know that Satan, a created being, is evil and exists prior to the fall of man. Scriptures do not explain how Satan became evil. They simply present him as evil and as God's opponent as he enters the stage in the drama of human life.

Satan's method of deceit sets the pattern for future deceptions. In the temptation (Gen 3:1–5) Satan entices Eve to eat of the forbidden Tree of the Knowledge of good and evil. God had set

---

1. Wolters, *Creation Regained*, 44.

this test so that Adam and Eve would know moral discernment at the highest level of obedience.

Satan asserted doubt concerning God's ways and he attacked God's character by implying that God was unfair. He focused on the negative. Eve succumbed to Satan's wiles. She misquoted God's permission, God's prohibition, and God's penalty. Satan responded by denying God's word. Satan essentially said, 1) You won't reap what you sow; 2) God fears, rather than loves man; 3) You can be independent of God; 4) There is efficacy in things; 5) Don't trust God's Word.

Satan succeeds in taking Eve's focus from God to self. Now that God is questioned, she trusts her own reasoning and Eve acts by sight rather than by faith. She sees; she covets; she takes; she draws others into sin. The consequences of sin (3:7–12) are separation, alienation, and anguish. There had been harmony between God and man; man and animals; man and land. Now harmony is gone as God's order is violated. The woman listens to Satan, the man listens to the woman, and the man attempts to have God listen to him.

What happened in the fall is summarized in the Westminster Catechism:

> 2. By this sin they fell from their original righteousness and communion with God, and so became dead in sin, and wholly defiled in all the parts and faculties of soul and body. 3. They being the root of all mankind, the guilt of this sin was imputed; and the same death in sin, and corrupted nature, conveyed to all their posterity descending form them by ordinary generation. 4. From this original corruption, whereby we are utterly indisposed, disabled, and made opposite to all good, and wholly inclined to all evil, do proceed all transgressions.[2]

Cornelius Plantinga defines sin as anything that violates the shalom that God intends. He says:

> In fact, we may safely describe evil as any spoiling of shalom, whether physically (e.g., disease), morally,

2. *Westminster Confession of Faith*, Chapter VI.

spiritually, or otherwise. Moral and spiritual evil are agential evil – that is, evil that, roughly speaking, only persons can do or have. Agential evil thus comprises evil acts and dispositions. Sin, then, is any agential evil for which some person (or group or persons) is to blame. In short, sin is culpable agential evil.[3]

The Relationship of Sin to Biblical Anthropology

When it comes to understanding the relationship of sin to biblical anthropology (study of mankind), we can see at least four stages suggested in Scripture.

(Stage One) Pre-Fall	(Stage Two) Fallen	(Stage Three) Redeemed	(Stage Four) Glorified
Created in the image of God	Effaced the image of God	Process of restoring the image of God	Full restoration of the image of God
Personality influenced by inner-life of God	Personality influenced by fallen Adamic nature	Personality influenced by Spirit of God (New Nature)	Personality influenced by Spirit of God
Personality influenced by righteous desires of the flesh	Personality influenced by unrighteous desires of the flesh	Personality influenced by unrighteous desires of the flesh	Personality influenced by redeemed and righteous flesh
Spiritual man in a sinless natural body	Natural man in a natural body	Spiritual man in a natural body	Spiritual man in a spiritual body

Sin in relation to Creation

A biblical view of the world and of the Christian's relationship to the world depends upon how one views sin in relation to creation.

3. Plantinga, *Not the Way It's Supposed to Be*, 14.

In Genesis 1–2 the created order is designated as good. Human sin does not exist within God's handiwork. "Sin, an alien invasion of creation, is completely foreign to God's purposes for his creation."[4] When sin entered through Satan's deception, all of creation became ensnared in the throes of abnormality and distortion.

However, Scripture does not teach that the goodness of creation was abolished by the fall or that creation is now identified with sin.

It is obvious to all that the fall affected the created world, culture, the institutions of creation such as marriage, bodily functions such as sexuality and eating, etc.

The distinction between the *structure* and *direction* of creation is helpful in understanding the relationship of sin to creation.

Structure refers to the order of creation as God intended it to be. *Structure* reflects the law of creation that the very nature (essence, substance) of something is what God created it to be. So we can think of things, humans, and institutions such as marriage in light of their structure and see their creational goodness. For instance, it is not the human, as a created being, that is evil but evil has distorted the way God intended humans to be. The created world is not evil but sin brings about the distortion of what God created. Sin is an alien invader into God's creation.

When we speak of the *direction* of creation, we refer to how God's order of creation is either distorted through the fall or it is redeemed and restored in Christ. When the biblical writers use the term "world" in a negative sense (Col 2:8; Rom 12:2; James 1:27; 2 Pet 2:20), they mean "the totality of unredeemed life dominated by sin outside of Christ." Christians who delimit some areas of the created world by calling them "worldly" or "secular" make a grave mistake, as if there is no worldliness in the church or there can be no holiness in the arts or politics. Many Christians have abandoned the "secular" realm and consequently the forces of evil often rule. Humans still have responsibility for the created order (*structure*) but this can be distorted by the fall or it can be redeemed and restored through Christ (*direction*).

4. Wolters, *Creation Regained*, 48.

From the fall of man on, all of future history and revelation is redemptive in nature. The effects of sin are so pervasive and powerful that only a divine solution will suffice. When you move from the fall in Genesis 3 to chapter 4, you immediately realize that sin has passed from parent to child. The story of Cain and Abel is not told to "warn us of the dangers of jealousy and hatred. Rather it shows the solidarity of the human race in Adam's sin (Rom 5:12–21); sin has been passed on to the next generation. Moreover, it demonstrates the alienation between an individual, his brother, and his God."[5]

The pervasive and powerful effects of sin as revealed in the history of Genesis 4–11 prepare us for God's sovereign intervention in the call of Abraham and the series of covenants that anticipate Jesus Christ, God's only solution for sin. All the distortion of God's created order (*structure*) and all distortion because of the fall (*direction*) are ultimately restored through God's Anointed, Jesus Christ. The complete restoration awaits the Consummation when sin and its effects will be removed (2 Pet 3:10–13; Rev 21:1–5).

This conviction that only Christ can fully restore a fallen creation and that only Christ can redeem and restore a fallen life keeps us dependent upon God and involved in prayer and evangelism. While we continue to bring Christ's redemption and restoration to bear upon the present created order, we do so knowing that the rule of Jesus Christ and the removal of sin is the ultimate solution.

> If man is basically good, or at least perfectible, apart from spiritual renewal, then the Christian approach to reformation of society will inevitably be primarily through government-sponsored education and civil legislation. If men are dead in trespasses and sins, darkened in their understanding, alienated from the life of God, because of the ignorance that is in them, then inevitably the Christian approach to society will be primarily through prayer and evangelism. If the sin that is in the world is mere creaturely limitation, ignorance, poor heredity, or bad government, the conclusions are the same. The Christian approach to society will be mainly by education and

5. Vangemeren, *Progress of Redemption*, 87.

legislation or perhaps attempted improvement of heredity through biological manipulation of conception.

But if the sin of the world is a form of bond-slavery to evil, evil in man himself constantly encouraged by demonic evil in the world itself, then the Christian's hope for cleansing the world's educational and legislative processes will be realistic as well as real. He will not expect to change the processes of society for the better apart from doing something to make men better.

This is to say that the Christian is certainly to approve indirect Christian social action through legislative and general educative processes. He also knows hopes for enduring improvement from these quarters are chimerical apart from bringing sizeable numbers of men into spiritual enlightenment. This is to say that prayer and evangelism in the context of vital evangelical Christianity must remain always at the heart of Christian social action.[6]

We move forward through the history of redemption, understanding at least these seven perspectives on the corruption of sin:

1. Human beings sinned, rebelled, and revolted against God's rule.

2. Individuals live continually between anguish and hope.

3. The nations live in a state of revolution against the Creator, but the Creator has limited the power of evil.

4. God rules over all the nations in grace and judgment.

5. God's concern with mankind is that of a grieved father, who works with his children to bring them to repentance. Responsibility lies with individuals.

6. The special blessing on humankind finds its focus in Shem, an ancestor of Abraham;

7. Israel's special position as an elect nation is an expression of God's free grace, whereby Israel is invited to the experience of restoration in Canaan by the glorious presence and blessing

6. Culver, *Civil Government*, 172.

of God, conditioned on its responsiveness to the Creator-Redeemer.[7]

The task of biblical theology is to show the way that God brings about the restoration of all things. God is still sovereign, and even human rebellion can never thwart his purpose. But this sovereign rule of God in a fallen universe needs to be distinguished from the kingdom of God. The kingdom is God's rule over his people in a realm in which all relationships are perfect. The fallen universe is the very opposite of the kingdom. Only through salvation will the kingdom be restored, for salvation is God bringing all things back to their right relationships.[8]

7. Vangemeren, *Progress of Redemption*, 96–97.

8. Goldsworthy, *According to Plan*, 140.

CHAPTER SIX

The Biblical Theme of Covenant[1]

Read: pages 154–200 in Goldsworthy, *According to Plan*.

The Old Testament Covenants

A STUDY of the covenants provides insight into God's temporal and ultimate purposes and how believers fit into those purposes. This study reveals the historical continuity and discontinuity between Israel and believers of this era, while affirming the original and ultimate unity of God's people and program and the common destiny of those people.

The major Old Testament covenants called by the Hebrew term *berith* are: (1) The Noahic Covenant; (2) the Abrahamic Covenant; (3) the Mosaic Covenant; (4) the Davidic Covenant; (5) the New Covenant.

Some would argue, not without some merit, of the existence of other covenants preceding the Noachic Covenant. They include a Convenient of Creation with Adam (Gen 1:26–28), a Covenant of works (Gen 2:8–9), and a Covenant of Grace (or Covenant of Commencement as others have called it) in Genesis 3:15. The

1. Much of this discussion on covenant is taken from the Th.M. thesis by this author entitled *A Critical Evaluation of the use of the Abrahamic Covenant in Dispensationalism* (Westminster Theological Seminary, 77–82).

37

language of the Covenant with Noah ("I establish [confirm] a covenant with you" Gen 9:9) possibly refers to what God says to Adam in Genesis 1–3.

All of these covenants are related to the original and ultimate purpose of God as revealed in Genesis 1:26–27. God's desire was and is to have a people who are like Him (seed) and who are blessed by Him (divine-human relationship) and who rule under Him in His world (land).

Sin temporarily disrupted this purpose, and, had not God acted in grace as manifested in these covenants, there would be no restoration to that original and ultimate purpose of God.

General Information on Covenants

This author defines covenant as "God's gracious gift to believing man by which God binds man to His eternal purposes."[2]

Though God is the initiator of all these covenants, four of them are unilateral (the basis for fulfillment is one person's obligation, God's), while one of them is bilateral (the covenant fulfillment is based on both parties being faithful to their obligations).

Three of the covenants—the Abrahamic, Davidic, and New—are clearly eternal, while one of them, the Mosaic, is conditioned on the response of the people, and one of the them, the Noahic, is concerned only with this present cosmos. Each of the covenants serves God's redemptive purposes.

What is the issue in a biblical covenant? Martens asserts "The issue of a covenant is not to establish a relationship, but to perpetuate it."[3] In some sense all of the covenants are built upon the relationship that inheres in God's creating man in His own image and giving him stewardship over the world. Dumbrell concurs noting that a covenant "gives quasi-legal backing to an arrangement which

2. See Lillback's discussion of the "The Mutual Binding of the Covenant" (Lillback, *Binding of God*, 273–76).

3. Martens, *God's Design*, 71.

is already in existence" and it "involves a solemn commitment by which a state of existing relationships is normalized."[4]

Due to the entrance of sin and the consequent marring of the relationship that man had with God at creation, Robertson's definition of covenant as "a bond-in-blood sovereignly administered"[5] further amplifies the understanding of covenant.

An Overview of the Covenants

The Noahic Covenant is a temporal, unilateral covenant of God's grace insuring that, even though similar conditions would exist for future world-wide judgment, God will guarantee the perpetuity of the race until the consummation of all things, especially His redemptive purposes.

The Abrahamic Covenant is an eternal, unilateral covenant of God's grace wherein He elects a man and his seed to be the temporal and eternal benefactors of the original and ultimate purpose of God.

The Mosaic Covenant is eternal in its substance, in that it reflects the holiness of God, but it is temporal in its mode of administration. It is a bilateral covenant of God's grace that set forth the conditions for the participation of Jacob's seed in the Abrahamic Covenant. External standards were given which bound the seed of Jacob to Yahweh the God of Abraham. On a national basis the experience of the blessings of the Abrahamic Covenant was contingent on national conformity to the Sinaitic Covenant. Assumed is the necessity of individual hearts that were circumcised to enable the keeping of the law (Deut 10:16). The standards of the Mosaic Covenant are obligatory for all saints, but the covenant itself lacks the strength to justify and sanctify. It anticipated the New Covenant mediated through Christ, who, through the Spirit, administers the covenant to the believer's life (Rom 7–8; 2 Cor 3).

---

4. Dumbrel, *Covenant and Creation*, 19.
5. Robertson, *Christ of the Covenants*, 15.

BIBLICAL THEMES

The Davidic Covenant is an eternal, unilateral covenant of God's grace that ties the fulfillment of God's original and ultimate purpose to one person, the Messianic King, the ideal representative seed of Abraham.

The New Covenant is an eternal, unilateral covenant of God's grace wherein the Abrahamic, Mosaic, and Davidic covenants converge. It ensures divine provision to meet the conditions necessary for participation in the original and ultimate purposes of God.

The Abrahamic, Mosaic, and Davidic especially anticipated Jesus Christ, who instituted the New Covenant. As the quintessential seed of Abraham, He is both the guarantor and inheritor of those former covenants. This fulfillment was initiated at the first advent of Jesus Christ, is presently experienced in the Church, and will be fully realized in the new heavens and earth.

Significant Points of the Covenants

The Noahic (Gen 6:17-8; 9:9-17)

The Noahic Covenant was given in a context where the condition of the world was characterized by "corrupt", which denotes " . . . the flagrant breach of a just order and particularly of an order divinely instituted."[6] The progression of sin culminated in "violence" which required the judgment of God by a worldwide flood.

As Dumbrell concludes,

> After the flood a covenant is instituted to guarantee to the world that even though sin would progress, resulting in a similar state of corruption, God will graciously insure the continued existence of the created order so that His purposes in redemption would be carried out.[7]

The Noahic Covenant prepares the way for the Abrahamic covenant in that it affirms that God's purposes continue to be of a world-wide nature. Dumbrell cogently observes:

6. Dumbrell, *Covenant and Creation*, 14.
7. Dumbrell, *Covenant and Creation*, 27.

40

We may take that the aim of this covenant is total harmony between man and his world. It may be a further and warranted inference, however, that the position of the bow as overarching, as it were, heavens and earth, speaks for the potential harmony of all creation under this arrangement.[8]

In the Noachic Covenant the value of human life and the centrality of man in accomplishing God's purpose is also highlighted. Man stands as "... the visible representative in the created world of the invisible God." He has what could be called "derived kingship"[9] and "... it is through man that divine purposes will be realized."[10]

This covenant shows us that "the world and man are part of one total divine construct and we cannot entertain the salvation of man in isolation from the world which he has affected."[11]

The Abrahamic Covenant (Gen 12:1–3,7)

The Abrahamic Covenant, couched in the setting of the Pentateuch, furnishes for that body of Scripture its theme,[12] as well as providing a theological track for the balance of Scriptures. In its literary context the Abrahamic Covenant follows on the heels of the Babel account and is intricately tied to it. At a time of ethnic, social, economic, and linguistic unity mankind cooperated in an effort to achieve what appears to be "... security through city building ... and the perpetuation of his generation ... through monumental works of architecture."[13]

8. Dumbrell, *Covenant and Creation*, 29.

9. Dumbrell, *Covenant and Creation*, 34.

10. Dumbrell, *Covenant and Creation*, 33.

11. Dumbrell, *Covenant and Creation*, 41.

12. David J. A. Clines suggests this theme of the books of Moses: "... the partial fulfillment--which implies also the partial non-fulfillment--of the promises to the patriarchs. The promise or blessing is both the divine initiative in a world where human initiatives always lead to disaster, and a re-affirmation of the primal divine intentions for man" (Clines, *Theme of the Pentateuch*, 29).

13. Dumbrell, *Covenant and Creation*, 59–60.

Babel was a search for a society with man at its center, not God. In a world that was to be a God-directed world, this was an arrogant human assertion.[14] As Dumbrell aptly observes concerning the dispersion: "The severity of the divine action would lead us to suppose that a gross and flagrant act of rebellion by mankind had been committed at Shinar."[15]

Instead of destroying the world as in Noah's day, God, having dispersed the world's population, now designs to reach them by graciously selecting and favoring Abraham and his seed with the end that the entire world would enjoy His blessing.

Accepting Genesis 1–11 as the background for the Abrahamic Covenant, the covenant, according to Dumbrell, provides " . . . a theological blueprint for the redemptive history of the world, a redemptive history which the call of Abraham sets in train."[16]

McComiskey concurs:

> [The promise given to Abraham] . . . comprises the heart of Biblical teaching regarding the people of God, for, besides affirming God's intent to form such a people, it serves to define the nature of that people in broad categories. The promise thus provides a *theological continuum* [emphasis mine] that spans all time.[17]

This covenant is Redemptive\Restorative in nature. It defines in detail the divine purpose of securing a seed, land, and divine-human relationship. It provides the blueprint by which God plans to bring about His original purpose for man and this world as initiated in the first chapter of Genesis and consummated in the last two chapters of Revelation.

---

14. Dumbrell, *Covenant and Creation*, 61.
15. Dumbrell, *Covenant and Creation*, 59.
16. Dumbrell, *Covenant and Creation*, 46.
17. McComiskey, *Covenants of Promise*, 58.

The Mosaic Covenant (Exodus 19–24)

The Mosaic Covenant is a bilateral covenant of God's grace of eternal substance though administered temporally.

> It establishes the conditions under which the terms of the promise could be maintained. The promise is the eternal expression of God's will. The law is the temporary framework that prescribed the terms of obedience for the people of God in the Mosaic era.[18]

The Mosaic Covenant reveals that " . . . Israel is the agent to achieve the wider purposes which the Abrahamic Covenant entails, purposes which involve the redemption of the whole world."[19] Dumbrell further notes that "the history of Israel from this point on is in reality merely a commentary upon the degree of fidelity with which Israel adhered to this Sinai-given vocation."[20]

The Mosaic Covenant revealed the holy standards expected of the people of God and the human inability of men to meet those conditions necessary to participate in the original and ultimate purpose of God. It forced men to cast themselves upon the grace and mercy of God. The Mosaic Covenant prepared for and anticipated the New Covenant.

In summary it can be said that the Mosaic Covenant offers an historical model of the expectations that God has for the people who will represent His name. It reminds all of the frailty and inability of man and causes men to anticipate, and now, to appreciate the grace of God as it is clearly expressed in the New Covenant.

The Davidic Covenant (2 Sam 7)

The Davidic Covenant is an eternal, unilateral covenant of God's grace that ties the fulfillment of God's original and ultimate purpose to one person, the Messianic King, the ideal seed of Abraham.

18. McComiskey, *Covenants of Promise*, 73.
19. Dumbrell, *Covenant and Creation*, 89.
20. Dumbrell, *Covenant and Creation*, 80.

It is through this king that the original purpose of God in Genesis 1–2 will be consummated. Under this Jewish king, God's chosen seed and the world will be restored to their original purposes under God.

The covenant as found in II Samuel 7:5–11 is called by Kaiser "the charter for humanity."[21] This idea is taken from the phrase in 2 Samuel 7:19 in the New King James Version: "And is this the manner of man, O, Lord God." This difficult Hebrew phrase, argues Kaiser, is best taken as an exclamation rather than an interrogative. The word from which "manner" is derived refers to the substance of what God has said. Kaiser quotes Eerdmann in regard to the antecedent: "It must be the *content* of the Lord's words about the future of his house that moves him, . . . not the *fact* that the Lord condescends to him . . . but *what* He has now *spoken* to him . . . This is the divine *torah* or prescription . . . for poor human creatures."[22] The Davidic covenant "prefigures in human terms the establishment of divine government through a human intermediary, so that the full intentions of the divine purpose for the race, expounded in Genesis 1–2, might be achieved."[23]

In this covenant David is promised a house (dynasty), a seed (posterity), a kingdom (kings, a dominion, a governed people), a son of God. "It anticipates one single Israelite who will ultimately qualify for such a relationship."[24] The elements of the Davidic Covenant have a striking similarity to the Abrahamic promise. Martens adds:

> This covenant holds out the hope of an age in which Israel will not be disturbed and in which the wicked will no more afflict them as formerly. The coming age of peace will, by inference, be linked to a Davidite.[25]

21. Kaiser, *Old Testament Theology*, 152.

22. Kaiser, *Old Testament Theology*, 154–55.

23. Dumbrell, *Covenant and Creation*, 152.

24. Kaiser, *Old Testament Theology*, 143–52.

25. Martens, *God's Design*, 134.

However, because of the repeated failures of the nation the expectation of the kingdom was translated by the prophets to an eschatological era. The prophets envisioned a continuing Davidic dynasty that found its expression in a king whose eternal reign will bring universal peace and justice. When a theological emergency was posed by the destruction of the two kingdoms, the prophets emerged with the message of an eschatological fulfillment.[26]

In the time of the destruction of the Northern kingdom Isaiah the prophet envisioned its future fulfillment. McComiskey said:

> [Isaiah foresaw] . . . a child to be born, whose government will have no end. His connection with the Davidic line is established by the association of his kingdom with the throne of David (9:7). His mediatorial function with regard to the promise is observable in his restoration of the land (9:1) and the security he gives his people (9:7). In 11:1, Isaiah spoke of the shoot from the stump of Jesse. This firmly establishes the Davidic origin of this figure who brings security to his people.[27]

Also, at the time of the dissolution of the southern kingdom, the prophet Jeremiah saw the fulfillment of the Davidic Covenant in "a righteous branch" (Jer 23:5-6) connected to the Davidic dynasty. He also in 33:14-22 saw that continuity between the Abrahamic and Davidic covenants is established. The prophet Amos "envisioned the return of the dynasty of David which would result in the return of Israel to their land, never again to be uprooted."[28]

The fact that the Davidic Covenant was purely a covenant of grace can be seen from the life of David himself and from the subsequent history of Israel. Kaiser observes:

> even though the anointed one himself became ensnared in his own lusts, humiliated by revolts from his own lusts, embarrassed by revolts from his own family, and cursed by others, God's guarantee still held . . . In the midst of

---

26. McComiskey, *Covenants of Promise*, 26.

27. McComiskey, *Covenants of Promise*, 26-27.

28. McComiskey, *Covenants of Promise*, 27.

human tragedy and failure, relentlessly, God's purpose and promise still went onward.[29]

The New Covenant (Jer 31:31–34)

The New Covenant is an eternal, unilateral covenant of God's grace contrasted to the Mosaic Covenant and, "implicitly also with the Abrahamic and Davidic covenants,"[30] in that it offers the permanent divine provision of forgiveness and the gift of the Spirit to meet the conditions necessary for participation in the original and ultimate purposes of God and to consummate those purposes.

The New Covenant was offered by both Ezekiel (36:24–37) and Jeremiah (31:31–40), who were prophets during and after the fall of Jerusalem. The fall of Samaria in 722 B.C. and the fall of Jerusalem in 586 B.C. were the final evidences of the inability of Israel to keep the Mosaic Covenant, the failure of the Davidic dynasty to be loyal to Yahweh, and the resulting disenfranchisement of Israel from the land promised in the Abrahamic Covenant.

In the New Covenant God was offering "the resources of His Spirit, so that this time the covenant partner would remain faithful, would exhibit the loyalty essential to covenant."[31] The purpose of this covenant as spelled out in Ezekiel 36:27 is to "move you to follow my decrees and be careful to keep my laws," i.e., the purpose was to elicit the obedience that God requires of those who will participate in the promise.

As the Mosaic Covenant elicited obedience through an external code of laws, now the New Covenant administrates an obedience which "is effected by the placing of the law within the heart and by the gracious work of the Holy Spirit."[32] One of the primary distinctions of the New Covenant is this radical inward change that becomes the driving force for obedience.

---

29. Kaiser, *Old Testament Theology*, 163–64.

30. Robertson, *Christ of the Covenants*, 281.

31. Martens, *God's Design*, 220–21.

32. McComiskey, *Covenants of Promise*, 163.

The New Covenant is related to the Abrahamic Covenant in that it explicates the terms by which one may participate in the Abrahamic promise. Furthermore, it not only sets forth the terms for participation, but also ensures that those terms will be met. It is "an instrument of grace, the terms of which are designed to aid the people under its administration to secure a spiritual inheritance."[33]

The New Covenant in contrast to the Mosaic Covenant does not necessitate a repeated sacrifice[34] nor a changing priesthood because both find their fulfillment in Jesus Christ.

The New Covenant relates to both Israel and believers of this dispensation. Because of the original and ultimate purpose of God to have one people for His name, presently individual Israelites, as well as any believing Gentile participate in the New Covenant promise.

While Pentecost signaled the beginning of this availability of the Spirit, the ultimate fulfillment of the New Covenant awaits the Consummation when God will bring about the restoration of all things.

Concerning the re-gathering of Israel, this author agrees with Martens:

> Even though the New Testament hope is on the church,
> the promise to Israel, while transmitted in large measure

---

33. McComiskey, *Covenants of Promise*, 165.

34. John Feinberg gives us four functions or usages of sacrifice the OT:

1. OT sacrifices served a governmental or theocratic function. Through sacrifice an Israelite maintained or restored his relationship within the theocracy. Often sin was a civil issue.

2. OT sacrifice had a typological function. They foreshadowed the coming sacrifice of Jesus Christ. We should not assume that their understanding of the typological function of sacrifice was as perceptual ours.

3. OT sacrifice served a function in worship. There were a number of offerings that were not atonement-related, but rather served as a means of worshipping God and bringing glory to Him.

4. OT sacrifices had a role in soteriology. Sacrifices were the natural outworking of saving faith in God. They relate more to the sanctification process than to the justification process (Feinberg, *Tradition and Testament*, 63–75).

to the church, is not for that reason exhausted but may quite conceivably find fulfillment on a historical plane.[35]

Our present participation in the New Covenant assures our future participation in that day. The New Covenant, as inaugurated in Jesus Christ (Lk 22:20), is the final point of convergence for the Abrahamic, Mosaic, and Davidic covenants.

35. Martens, *God's Design*, 259.

CHAPTER SEVEN

The Biblical Theme of the Church

(The People of God)

Read: pages 201–32 in Goldsworthy, *According to Plan*.

The OT concept of the People of God

THE PEOPLE of God are a people in community with each other and in community with God. The people of God at Creation were Adam and Eve. As we have seen, they were created for Sonship and Stewardship. The fall disrupted the community of the people of God with each other and with God. The words of God's curse on Satan make clear that from that time forth there would be a conflict between two corporate entities (two peoples) – the seed of the woman and the seed of Satan. These corporate entities would have two main representatives – Satan and Jesus.

Chapters 3–11 of Genesis record the rebellion and division rather than the obedience and harmony of those whom God created to fellowship with Himself. Apart from a few individuals and their families, the earth had become corrupt. The events of the flood and Babel prepare the way for the call of Abraham. In the accounts of the flood and Babel, human wickedness and rebellion is the cause for God's judgment. Both of these events are somewhat typological of the eschatological salvation and judgment of the world.

Prior to Genesis 12 God's dealing had largely been with individuals. The Abrahamic covenant introduces the concept of a "corporate seed", i.e., "the people of God."

As the concept of "the people of God" emerges in the OT, it becomes clear that the main identifying feature of the people of God has always been "faith." This is most clear in the account of Abraham (Gen 15:6), though it was also true of those prior to Abraham according to Hebrews 11.

The People of God are the Seed of Abraham by Faith

The Abrahamic covenant often speaks of "seed." The Hebrew word and the related Greek word present a complex concept in identifying the recipients of the Abrahamic promise. "Seed" is used at times to include (1) the physical descendants of Abraham, (2) those who share the faith of Abraham, whether physical seed or not, and (3) in Galatians 3:16, Paul argues forcefully that "seed" in the singular finds its ultimate reference to Christ as "the" offspring of Abraham.

This varied usage produces perplexity in understanding "who are the recipients of the Abrahamic covenant?" Part of the solution to this complexity is to understand that "seed" is used to describe both a singular entity as well as a collective one.

The promise was given to Abraham and to his seed (Gen 12:1–3,7; 15; 17:1–22; 22:15–18), i.e., both to Isaac (27:27–29) and to Jacob (28:10–15). Both Isaac and Jacob stood representatively in the Messianic office, an office fulfilled in Jesus Christ. McComiskey notes: "The collective function of "seed" allows the writer to refer to the group or to a representative individual of the group."[1] The focus is not only on the physically related "seed," for those who are not physically related can participate in the covenant (Gen 17:9–14). The collective singular disallows any notion of "seeds,"

1. McComiskey, *Covenants of Promise*, 20.

physical and spiritual. There is but one seed. The New Testament clarifies that Jesus Christ is the ideal representative seed, while those in Christ comprise the collective seed, i.e., the community of faith (Gal 3:16,29). Isaac and Jacob cannot ultimately fulfill the promise. Only Jesus Christ can bless the earth in a final sense. The collective seed have no identity apart from their relationship to the ideal representative, Jesus Christ.

This dual concept of "individual representative" and "corporate community of faith" is essential to understanding "seed" and its relationship to the people of God. It appears that later in the progress of revelation the Davidic covenant expands on the royal status of the representative individual who guarantees the covenant, and the New Covenant expands on the spiritual nature of the corporate community of faith who participate in that covenant.

As mentioned earlier, another step in resolving the complexity of "seed" is to understand that "seed" does not equate to "physical descendants." Though Ishmael was a descendant of Abraham, he was not the seed of Abraham to whom the promise was guaranteed. Likewise, Esau was a descendant of Isaac, yet was not in the line of promise. Also, there were many that were physically seed of Abraham through Isaac and Jacob, yet who stood outside the covenant (Rom 2:28–29).

Clearly, not all of the physical "seed" of Abraham inherit the promise. Only those physical descendants bound in a unique "faith" relationship or those non-physical "seed" who by faith enter that covenant of Abraham inherit the promise.

The unique relationship that establishes any man as a true seed of Abraham is one built on a faith participation in a divinely initiated covenant.[2] O. Palmer Robertson recognizes covenant as the bond that determines relations between God and his people:

> By creation God bound himself to man in covenantal relationship. After man's fall into sin, the God of all creation graciously bound himself to man again by committing himself to redeem a people to himself from

2. See Robertson, "Genesis 15:6," 259–89.

lost humanity. From creation to consummation the covenantal bond has determined the relation of God to his people.[3]

Daniel P. Fuller in his discussion of the seed of Abraham concludes that since faith is the prerequisite for participation in the Abrahamic covenant by both Jew and Gentile, then "faith which produces obedience, rather than physical descent, is the primary aspect of the seed of Abraham."[4]

It holds true then that physically related "seed" are not guaranteed participation in the Abrahamic promise, but the promise is ensured "to all the people of faith throughout all ages."[5] Once again, the New Testament affirms that not all Israelites were inheritors of the promise (Rom 2:28–29) and that some of those outside Abraham's physical seed do inherit the promise (Gal 3:29).

The "seed" of Abraham are those who by faith engage the "The Seed", whether physically related or not.

The People of God have a unique relationship to God and to the nations.

The Abrahamic Covenant makes clear that God calls a people to Himself so that they can mediate His blessing of redemption to the nations of the world. The purpose of God's blessing on Abraham is that Abraham would be a blessing to the world. The three promises to Abraham are followed by an imperative to Abraham.

> 2 "I will make you into a great nation and I will bless you;
> I will make your name great, and you will be a blessing.
> 3 I will bless those who bless you, and whoever curses you I will curse; and all peoples on earth will be blessed through you" (Gen 12:2–3).

God filled Abraham with life that he in turn might mediate life to others, i.e., God blessed Abraham so that Abraham would

---

3. Robertson, *Christ of the Covenants*, 25.
4. Fuller, *Hermeneutics of Dispensationalism*, 234.
5. McComiskey, *Covenants of Promise*, 17.

obey God. Verse three describes how God will fulfill this purpose: "I will bless those who bless you, and whoever curses you I will curse." The additional promise: "and all peoples on earth will be blessed through you," contrary to the translation in the New International Version, wherein "will be blessed" is taken as a passive, is better translated as "find for themselves a blessing."[6] This line of the covenant delineates the universal scope of God's redemptive and restorative program for the world.

Exodus 19 reveals that the election of Israel was an election to be a missionary nation with a world-wide impact.

> 1 In the third month after the Israelites left Egypt-- on the very day-- they came to the Desert of Sinai. 2 After they set out from Rephidim, they entered the Desert of Sinai, and Israel camped there in the desert in front of the mountain. 3 Then Moses went up to God, and the LORD called to him from the mountain and said, "This is what you are to say to the house of Jacob and what you are to tell the people of Israel: 4 'You yourselves have seen what I did to Egypt, and how I carried you on eagles' wings and brought you to myself. 5 Now if you obey me fully and keep my covenant, then out of all nations you will be my treasured possession. Although the whole earth is mine, 6 you will be for me a kingdom of priests and a holy nation.' These are the words you are to speak to the Israelites."

Dumbrell cogently discusses the significance of these concepts in their Old Testament context. The word "possession" (*segullah*) derives from an Akkadian term which refers "to what is owned personally or what has carefully been put aside for personal use."[7] It is a term that is nuanced by its use in suzerain\vassal relationships.

The Hebrew words "kingdom of priests" describe the mediatorial function of the nation. In an ancient society the priest was separated from the people in order to serve them. The separation

---

6. Dumbrell, *Covenant and Creation*, 70–71.

7. Dumbrell, *Covenant and Creation*, 85.

of the people was a demonstration of their allegiance to the covenant. Israel was to serve the world by being distinct from it.

By this new relationship, as disclosed in these terms, Israel is "withdrawn from the sphere of common international contact and finds her point of contact as a nation in her relationship to Yahweh."[8] Under this new constitution she becomes "a societary model for the world. She will provide, under the direct rule which the covenant contemplates, the paradigm of the theocratic rule which is to be the biblical aim of the whole world."[9]

This identity of the people of God as a missionary nation is carried through the OT into the New (Matt 28:18–20; 1 Pet 2:9–10).

The People of God are a Holy People

The people of the covenant-making God are to reflect the character and acts of their God. Their call is to "'Be holy, as I am Holy,' says the Lord" (Lev 11:44–45; 1 Pet 1:15–16). The purpose of holiness is that the Holy God may dwell in the midst of His people.

The OT law set forth an external standard of holiness. Conformity to this law was the basis of blessing or cursing. Jesus is the end of the law to everyone who believes. He embodied the holiness that God required. He fulfilled all the types and foreshadowing that existed in the holiness code. He imputes righteousness to those who repent of their sin and trust in Him.

The royal law of the NT is the internalized law of love (James 2:8; Mark 12:29–31; Rom 13:8). This does not mean that love for God was absent in the life of an OT believer (Deut 6:4–5) or that law serves no purpose in the life of a NT believer (John 14:15). Jesus Christ instituted the New Covenant that internalizes the law of God in one's heart, while the Covenant of Moses is fulfilled and abrogated in Christ (2 Corinthians; Hebrews).

---

8. Dumbrell, *Covenant and Creation*, 87.
9. Dumbrell, *Covenant and Creation*, 87.

The distinguishing marks of holiness that define the people of God today are the moral and ethical teaching of Scripture, the gospel of Jesus Christ, the authority of Scripture as a way of life, and their likeness to God[10] in displaying the fruit of the Spirit which is a reflection of the moral attributes of God.

The People of God are One in Christ
(Selected New Testament Texts)

Romans 4

In this chapter the apostle continues his argument that justification is by faith alone. It is faith, not rite or law that establishes man in relationship to God. He illustrates from the experience of Abraham to whom justification was granted prior to the requirement of the rite of circumcision. The apostle contends that circumcision was not the link between Abraham and those who participated in the covenant with him, but rather "faith" was that link (Rom 4:9–12). Circumcision merely portrayed that faith.

He further asserts that Abraham received the promise by faith prior to the giving of the law (Rom 4:13–15). Paul here understands the Abrahamic promise as primarily having redemptive significance.

His conclusion is that the promise comes by faith and that those who share Abraham's faith are related to the promise. "He is the father of us all" and the promise is "guaranteed to all Abraham's offspring" (Rom 4:16).

In quoting Genesis 17:3 Paul equates the Gentile believers of Rome with the "many nations" of the Abrahamic covenant. Both Genesis 17 and Romans 4 make no distinction between the "many nations" and the "seed of Abraham." Abraham is the father of both. Romans 4 shows that Genesis 17 anticipated that "seed of Abraham" and "many nations" involved, not physical descent, but a relationship of faith.

---

10. When we speak of our likeness to God we do not mean "identical" but rather "patterned after."

Romans 9–11

This passage is critical to any interpretation of the Abrahamic Covenant because it concerns the apparent failure of the covenant promises to the nation of Israel. The apostle's explanation of God's past, present, and future relation to Israel sheds light on the intent and scope of the Abrahamic Covenant.

In brief, Romans 9 dispels the notion that physical descendance constitutes Israel as the people of God and clarifies the true nature of that people. Using both the choice of Isaac over Ishmael in 9:6–9 and the choice of Jacob over Esau in 9:10–13, Paul argues that Abraham's true offspring are the those who inherit the promise (v.8) and that those inheritors of the promise become such through their faith participation (9:30–10:21) in the sovereign plan of God (9:1–21).

God's plan to gather a people for Himself also includes those Gentiles who share that faith response (9:22–26; 10:12–13). This inclusion of Gentiles is not to be perceived as a rejection of ethnic Israel. Though ethnicity in itself does not guarantee participation in the purposes of God, God's present extension of His grace to the nations does not exclude the availability of His grace to ethnic Israel (11:1).

The salvation of any Israelite, such as Paul (11:1–2), Elijah (11:2–6), or Jews today, demonstrates God's faithfulness to His promises to ethnic Israel. God's present abrogation of Israel's favored nation status and his glorious work among the nations, serve the dual purpose of saving Gentiles and arousing envy in Israelites.

However, the present extension of God's mercy to the Gentiles should not be construed as a negation of His promises for Israelites.[11] The partial hardening of Jews and the fullness of the Gentiles is the manner[12] in which God is accomplishing the saving of Israel. This is consistent with the Scripture that anticipated the

11. See the discussion of Rom 11:11–32 defending a future for Israel (Andrews, *Th.M. Thesis.*).

12. *houtos* is here used with the sense of "in this way" (Arndt and Gingrich, *Greek - English Lexicon,* 602). As in its two other occurrences in this chapter (vv.5, 31), it describes the manner in which something takes place.

coming of the Deliverer to Sion to take away sins. The Deliverer has come and is now gathering both Jew and Gentile unto Himself (11:25- 27). Some, such as Martin Wouldstra, argue that the "saving of all Israel" in Romans 9 is presently being accomplished through the formation into one body of both Jew and Gentile and that Israel " . . . will not form a separate program or a separate entity next to the church."[13]

The olive tree illustration sets forth the unity and continuity of the people of God. As the ingrafting of Gentiles does not replace the original branches, so the ingrafting of Israelites will not supplant the position of Gentiles.

The apostle's understanding of God's past, present, and future work among the nations and Israel coincides with the understanding that "the undeniable center of Old Testament religion lies in the believer's response to the words of the covenant God that He would be Abraham's God and the God of his descendants."[14] Included in those descendants are all those who have faith in Abraham's God.

Galatians 3

In the apostle's discussion of the relationship of the law to saving faith, he introduces Abraham as a paradigm of saving faith and inclusion in the promises of God. In the course of his discussion the apostle makes some interpretive statements, based on his understanding of the Genesis passages, that reflect on the Abrahamic Covenant. These statements are:

1. "those who believe are children of Abraham" (v.7);

2. "The Scripture foresaw that God would justify the Gentiles by faith, and announced the gospel in advance to Abraham: "All nations will be blessed through you" (v.8);

3. "those who have faith are blessed along with Abraham" (v.9);

---

13. Wouldstra, *Israel and the Church*, 236–37.
14. Wouldstra, *Israel and the Church*, 227.

4. "He redeemed us in order that the blessing given to Abraham might come to the Gentiles through Jesus Christ" (v.14);

5. "The promises were spoken to Abraham and to his seed. The Scripture does not say 'and to seeds,' meaning many people, but 'and to your seed,' meaning one person, who is Christ" (v.16);

6. "But the Scripture declares that the whole world is a prisoner of sin, so that what was promised, being given through faith in Jesus Christ, might be given to those who believe" (v.22).

Paramount in these verses is the redemptive significance of the Abrahamic Covenant as it finds its consummation in the person of Jesus Christ. Christ as the quintessential seed of Abraham is both the guarantor and inheritor of the promises of the covenant.

Relationship with Christ, established by emulating the faith of Abraham, guarantees one's participation in the promises of the covenant. It is not the keeping of the law nor physical descendance from Abraham that constitutes one as a child of Abraham, but rather faith in Jesus Christ.

These verses sanction the redemptive nature of the Abrahamic Covenant. They confirm that covenant as the unifying factor between Jews and Gentiles and they substantiate the view that there is one people of God of all ages that share the covenants of Scripture which find their consummation in Christ.

Strikingly, Paul perceives redemption in Christ to be the dominant, though probably not exclusive, feature of the Abrahamic Covenant. He finds the consummation of the covenant in Christ and participation in the covenant to be predicated on relationship to Christ. Though admittedly an argument from silence, the "earthly" nature of the promises to Abraham appears to be somewhat idealized in Christ. Though not necessarily eviscerating those "earthly" elements of the Abrahamic Covenant, it certainly places them in a new light.

Ephesians 2:11–22

This pericope offers a contrast between Gentiles apart from Christ (2:12) and Gentiles in Christ (2:13). In delineating that contrast, Paul asserts the unity and continuity of the people of God.

In the past Gentiles were able to participate in the covenants of God only through their identification with the God of Israel and their becoming proselytes of the religion of Israel. The advent of Christ ushered in a marked change in the focus of redemption.

No longer does common participation in the religion of Israel guarantee one's participation in the covenants, but rather common participation in the Lord Jesus Christ (the true Israel?) binds one to the covenants of promise.

Formerly, Gentiles apart from Christ were "excluded from citizenship in Israel and foreigners to the covenants of the promise" (2:12); whereas now, Gentiles in Christ "are no longer foreigners and aliens, but fellow citizens with God's people and members of God's household" (2:19).

The dividing wall (2:14) between Jew and Gentile is destroyed through the person and work of Jesus Christ. A new order has been established, replacing the old and forbidding its reconstruction.

The temple of Judaism is now replaced with a temple composed of Jew and Gentile sharing alike the life of the Spirit (2:21–2). Paul interprets the present experience of believing Jews and Gentiles in Christ as that which was anticipated by the covenants.

1 Peter 2:9–10

This text assigns the elevated status granted to Israel in Exodus 19:5–6 to New Testament believers. In unmistakable language—" a chosen people, a royal priesthood, a holy nation, a people belonging to God" (1 Pet 2:9), Peter removes any thought of a continuing distinction between Jew and Gentile, formerly marked by supremacy of the nation of Israel.

Furthermore, "now, the people of God" (2:10) becomes the designation that Peter grants to New Testament believers, echoing the words of Hosea the prophet (Hos 2:23).

Conclusion

Due to the advent of Christ, as the seed of Abraham, the New Testament text reveals a semi-realized fulfillment of the Abrahamic covenant in New Testament believers.

The texts that consider the question of "who are the people of God?" unequivocally answer "all of those who are in Christ Jesus." In reference to the unity of believing Jews and Gentiles, George N. H. Peters cogently concludes:

> Both elect are the seed, the children of Abraham; both sets of branches are on the same stock, on the same root, on the same olive tree; both constitute the same Israel of God, the members of the same body, fellow-citizens of the same commonwealth; both are Jews 'inwardly' (Romans 2:29), and of the true 'circumcision' (Phil. 3:3), forming the same 'peculiar people,' 'holy nation,' and 'royal priesthood'; both are interested in the same promises, covenants, and kingdom; both inherit and realize the same blessings at the same time.[15]

The church today is the living representation of Christ to the world. It is His covenant community bound together by the Spirit of truth. It is His militant kingdom set in the midst of the alien kingdom of darkness. The church is destined to triumph just as Christ has triumphed over sin and death.

---

15. Peters, *Theocratic Kingdom*, 404.

CHAPTER EIGHT

The Biblical Theme of
the Consummation

Read: pages 233–303 in Goldsworthy, *According to Plan.*

FROM THE beginning God has had the end in view. All of OT history anticipated a day (later called "the day of the Lord") when God would consummate His redemptive/restoration and judgment of man and the world. The "day of the Lord" (*Yom Yahweh*) first emerges in the Old Testament prophet Amos in the eight century B.C. During the economic revival in Israel under Jereboam II the nation had come to believe that things would keep getting better for them, despite their lack of allegiance to Yahweh. In Amos and other prophets (like Zephaniah) *Yom Yahweh* takes on eschatological overtones of wrath "against their popular expectations of a more glorious future, Amos describes the terror of God's involvement in human affairs."[1]

Earlier in her history, Israel had a horizontal view of the kingdom in which they as a nation expected the blessings, promises, and covenantal benefits to naturally keep increasing. They assumed that their position among the nations would be enhanced. Unfortunately, they did not give adequate attention to the commitment and response that the Lord required of them. The prophets

---

1. VanGemeren, *Progress of Redemption*, 450.

introduce the radical teaching that God will preserve a remnant, that the Lord himself will establish His kingdom by a vertical intrusion, and that the nations and Israel would suffer judgment.

Almost always *Yom Yahweh* describes what we might call a redemptive/judgment motif. In *Yom Yahweh* some are being judged and others are being delivered. Sometimes judgment is upon the enemies of Israel and Israel is delivered. At other times judgment is upon Israel and a remnant is delivered.

VanGemeren offers the acrostic of the word "TRUMPET" to show a fuller dimension of *Yom Yahweh*.[2]

Total Restoration

It is within the world of creation that redemption takes place. As we saw earlier in our discussion on Creation, "Scripture does not teach that the goodness of creation was abolished by the fall or that creation is now identified with sin." We can avoid an unhealthy pessimism regarding this world be remembering that "Redemption is not a deliverance from the material world but the reestablishment and sanctification of it."[3] The Bible does not support a dualistic view of the world in which God must destroy it because it is evil. Though the form of this world must pass away (1 Cor 7:31), God will transform it into a holy habitation for the saints of God (2 Pet 3:13).

On the other hand we avoid an overly optimistic view of the world by remembering the future intrusion of God's judgment. We live with the tension of being part of the new creation while being present on an unredeemed earth. We are called to be salt, light, and agents of transformation in subduing the earth by living up to Christ's expectations of righteousness, justice, love, and peace. However, we also recognize that "the world and its structures must fall."[4]

2. The discussion that follows is heavily dependent on VanGemeren, *Progress of Redemption*, 448–64.

3. VanGemeren, *Progress of Redemption*, 450.

4. VanGemeren, *Progress of Redemption*, 452.

Even our anticipation of the resurrection of our bodies "affirms the inherent goodness of the material order, when renewed by the power and salvation of God."[5]

The death and resurrection of Jesus Christ ultimately assure the restoration of all things.

Rule of God

As we have seen, "kingdom" or the "rule of God" is a basic theme of Biblical theology. In Genesis 1 God is presented as the Creator/King and humans as vice-regents. Goldsworthy at the end of each chapter adequately shows the development of the kingdom in each stage of biblical revelation. The Lord is not only Creator and Redeemer; He is King. As VanGemeren notes, 'The great King rules in judging and avenging His enemies and delivering and vindicating His people."[6]

One of the ways that Yahweh is revealed in the OT is as the Divine Warrior. Tremper Longman suggests that there are five phases of divine warfare.[7]

Phases of Divine Warfare					
		Christ's First Coming		Christ's Second Coming	
Phase One God's fight against flesh and blood enemies of Israel	Phase Three Postexilic anticipation of the Divine Warrior		Phase Four Christ against Satan		Phase Five The final battle
Phase Two					
God's fight against Israel					

---

5. VanGemeren, *Progress of Redemption*, 452.

6. VanGemeren, *Progress of Redemption*, 435.

7. Longman, *Making Sense*, 79.

Unbroken Covenants – Creation and Redemption

As we saw in the discussion on covenants, the major covenants (Noahic, Abrahamic, Mosaic, Davidic, and New) converge in Jesus Christ. Though He has come and has set in motion the "last days", we yet anticipate a consummate fulfillment. On the basis of the Noahic Covenant we expect the transformation of creation, involving blessing, harmony, and the integration of creation and redemption. In the Abrahamic Covenant we expect the vindication of His choice of Israel and the presence of God among people of all nations. In the Davidic Covenant we anticipate victory, glory, and peace under the rule of Messiah, the Son of David. In the New Covenant we expect that all that believe will fully share in the covenant promises.

Messianic Blessing

God will establish a kingdom of peace, justice, righteousness, blessing and prosperity for His people. This kingdom will be under the Davidic Messiah, the Root of Jesse (Isa 9:2–7; Jer 33:14–26). Zechariah presents the lowliness of this king as he rides on a donkey (Zech 9:9).

Isaiah presents the Messiah as one who suffers (Isa 53).

Throughout the OT we often see this shift between the Divine Warrior who conquers and transforms, a human, priestly Messiah (Ps 110; Jer. 33:22), and Messiah who is the Son of God (Ps 2) appointed to subdue all nations. The presence of the messianic kingdom is in Jesus Christ. The future establishment of His kingdom will manifest the rule of God more than any previous time. The hope of the saints to enjoy this Messianic rule lies in Jesus Christ.

People of God Renewed

Ever since the fall of Adam and Eve, God has been redeeming a people for Himself out of all humankind. The Old Testament people of God enjoyed the presence of God in the temple. They experienced revelations of His glory. They were given assurance of their special status of their being adopted as children of God. They had guarantees of a glorious future. They received forgiveness. They experienced special joys in life. Yet, they anticipated a greater salvation and permanent liberation from their enemies.

The New Testament people of God realize clearly that all of the benefits that God brings to His people are rooted in the atoning death and resurrection of the Messiah. Both the OT prophets and Jesus agree with God's original intent that His people should give loyalty, love, submission, and commitment to His kingdom rather than to any earthly kingdom. The new Jerusalem depicts the saints living in righteous, peaceful, loving, joyful fellowship fulfilling the expectation that God originally gave to Abraham: "Walk before me and be blameless" (Gen 17:1).

Enemies Avenged

Our expectation is more than a personal one; it is one that longs for the vindication of the righteousness of God throughout the whole world. Our hope is in God's justice. The final judgments will both vindicate the righteous and indict the ungodly. "The new world belongs to the righteous who have been persecuted, oppressed, maligned, and unjustly dealt with in life. The righteous cry out for justice and thirst for righteousness, awaiting the full establishment of God's righteousness and justice."[8]

Paul describes that day in these terms and encourages suffering Christians:

> 4 Therefore, among God's churches we boast about your perseverance and faith in all the persecutions and trials you are enduring. 5 All this is evidence that God's judgment is right, and as a result you will be counted worthy of the kingdom of God, for which you are suffering. 6 God is just: He will pay back trouble to those who trouble you 7 and give relief to you who are troubled, and to us as well. This will happen when the Lord Jesus

8. Vangemeren, *Progress of Redemption*, 458.

is revealed from heaven in blazing fire with his powerful
angels. 8 He will punish those who do not know God
and do not obey the gospel of our Lord Jesus. 9 They will
be punished with everlasting destruction and shut out
from the presence of the Lord and from the majesty of
his power 10 on the day he comes to be glorified in his
holy people and to be marveled at among all those who
have believed. This includes you, because you believed
our testimony to you (2 Thess 1).

Transformation by the Spirit

Today the Spirit of God is preparing the church for final glory. As
the Apostle Paul says:

> 17 Now the Lord is the Spirit, and where the Spirit of the
> Lord is, there is freedom. 18 And we, who with unveiled
> faces all reflect the Lord's glory, are being transformed
> into his likeness with ever-increasing glory, which comes
> from the Lord, who is the Spirit (2 Cor 3).

The Spirit is the firstfruits of the age to come (Eph 1:13–14).
His presence and work in our lives keeps us moving toward that
day of total transformation, when the Spirit will renew all things
(Isa 32:15; 44:3). Richard Gaffin aptly comments: "In the 'firstfruits' power of Pentecost the church lives eloquently in the hope
of the glory to be revealed (Rom 8:18–23). Confident the expectation of a new heavens and a new earth in which righteousness
dwells (2 Pet 3:13)."[9]

Perspectives on the Consummation

Because the OT believer anticipated the future coming of the Messiah, he viewed time in the following manner:

9. Gaffin, *Resurrection and Redemption*, 15.

		Midpoint of History	
Between Creation ------	---- and Consummation		After the Consummation
Creation	OT Believer	The Coming of Christ	Consummation

From a NT perspective, we know that Christ has come and is coming again. In some sense the consummation has begun. We live in days of "realized eschatology" as well as being expectant of "future eschatology." This is what some have called the "already, not yet" approach to eschatology or "two-age eschatology." All of these terms indicate that in some way, the incarnation, death, and resurrection of Jesus Christ initiates the beginning of the end. His death and resurrection defeated the evil powers. Christ has won the victory. Though we continue to "fight the good fight," we know that the war is won. Oscar Cullman draws a parallel from someone living between D-day and V-day during WWII and how a NT believer lives between the victory won at Calvary and the consummation of that victory at the return of Christ.

> The decisive battle in a war may have already occurred in a relatively early stage of the war, and yet the war still continues. Although the decisive effect of that battle is perhaps not recognized by all, it nevertheless already means victory. But the war must still be carried on for an undefined time, until 'Victory Day.' Precisely this is the situation of which the New Testament is conscious, as a result of the recognition of the new division of time; the revelation consists precisely in the fact of the proclamation that that event on the cross, together with the resurrection which followed, was the already concluded decisive battle[10].

Consequently, the New Testament believer views time as follows:

10. Cullman, *Christology*, 84.

		Midpoint of History		2nd Coming of Christ

		Midpoint of History		2nd Coming of Christ
	OT Believer	1st Coming of Christ	NT Believer	
Creation				Final Consummation

For the OT believer the great mid-point of human history (what our calendars indicate as B.C. and A.D.) was future. To NT believers the great mid-point is past. Geerhardus Vos offers a helpful chart to illustrate these two different eschatological outlooks:

		OT Scheme	
This age >>>>>>>	>>>>>>>>>>>>>>>	>>>>>>>>>>>>>>	The Age to Come
		NT Scheme	
	Resurrection of Jesus	>>>>>>>>>>>>>>	The Coming
	The World to Come realized in Principle	>>>>>>>>>>>>>>	Future age and world realized in solid existence
	(in heaven) (on earth)	>>>>>>>>>>>>>>	
	This age	>>>>>>>>>>>>>>	

The New Testament believer lives in both this age and as well the age to come. In some sense he is already "seated in the heavenlies with Christ" though still very much present in this world.

God has always intended to consummate all things in Jesus Christ. Jesus is the end (*telos*) and the last thing (*eschaton*) to which all history has been moving. This end includes the first and second coming of Christ, the defeat of Satan and removal of evil, the resurrection and judgment of the just and unjust, the mediatorial kingdom and eternal rule of Jesus Christ, and the new heavens and new earth.

I have purposely avoided offering any detailed schematic system of the end times attempting to keep the big picture in mind. All evangelical Christians hold a form of eschatology that is Christ-centered. Though schematics can be developed by collating and comparing Scriptures, all schematic systems are somewhat tentative, since no OT or NT author found it necessary to lay out a detailed schematic. Though personally I am amillennial in my understanding of Scripture, I agree with the conclusion of Vangemeren:

> Regrettably, evangelical Christians have locked horns on the precise details of the precise details of interpretation and, even more regrettably, have defined Evangelicalism in terms of a particular millennial perspective. Each of the millennial positions suffers from not hearing the whole prophetic and apostolic witness. Out of concern for the total witness, we must strive for unity even while recognizing diversity. Christ calls us to persevere in living our lives as Christians in preparation for the blessed hope. Our calling is not to work out the details of the Blessed Hope.[11]

> 15 According to the Lord's own word, we tell you that we who are still alive, who are left till the coming of the Lord, will certainly not precede those who have fallen asleep. 16 For the Lord himself will come down from heaven, with a loud command, with the voice of the archangel and with the trumpet call of God, and the dead in Christ will rise first. 17 After that, we who are still alive and are left will be caught up together with them in the clouds to meet the Lord in the air. And so we will be with the Lord forever. 18 Therefore encourage each other with these words (1 Thess 4).

---

11. Vangemeren, *Progress of Redemption*, 474.

Conclusion

THE SUPERIOR glory of Jesus Christ shines through all of the themes of Scripture.

In Christ we see the superior glory of the Triune God.

¹⁴ And the Word became flesh and dwelt among us, and we have seen his glory, glory as of the only Son from the Father, full of grace and truth (John 1:14).

⁶ For God, who said, "Let light shine out of darkness," has shone in our hearts to give the light of the knowledge of the glory of God in the face of Jesus Christ (2 Cor 4:6)

In Creation we see the superior glory of his power and wisdom.

¹In the beginning was the Word, and the Word was with God, and the Word was God. ² He was in the beginning with God. ³ All things were made through him, and without him was not anything made that was made (John 1:1–3)

"Worthy are you, our Lord and God, to receive glory and honor and power, for you created all things, and by your will they existed and were created (Rev 4:11)

In the Consummation we see the superior glory of his triumph over sin, death, and Satan.

[11] Then I looked, and I heard around the throne and the living creatures and the elders the voice of many angels, numbering myriads of myriads and thousands of thousands, [12] saying with a loud voice,
> "Worthy is the Lamb who was slain,
> to receive power and wealth and wisdom and might
> and honor and glory and blessing!"

[13] And I heard every creature in heaven and on earth and under the earth and in the sea, and all that is in them, saying,
> "To him who sits on the throne and to the Lamb
> be blessing and honor and glory and might forever and ever!" (Rev 5:11–13).

[22] And I saw no temple in the city, for its temple is the Lord God the Almighty and the Lamb. [23] And the city has no need of sun or moon to shine on it, for the glory of God gives it light, and its lamp is the Lamb (Rev 21:22)

In Corruption we the superior glory of his obedience and atonement as the Second Adam.

[18] Therefore, as one trespass led to condemnation for all men, so one act of righteousnessleads to justification and life for all men. [19] For as by the one man's disobedience the many were made sinners, so by the one man's obedience the many will be made righteous (Rom 5:18–19).

[9] For if there was glory in the ministry of condemnation, the ministry of righteousness must far exceed it in glory. [10] Indeed, in this case, what once had glory has come to have no glory at all, because of the glory that surpasses it (2 Cor 3:9–10).

In the Covenants we the superior glory of his being the quintessential seed of Abraham in whom all of the promises of God converge.

¹³ Christ redeemed us from the curse of the law by becoming a curse for us—for it is written, "Cursed is everyone who is hanged on a tree"— ¹⁴ so that in Christ Jesus the blessing of Abraham might come to the Gentiles, so that we might receive the promised Spirit through faith (Gal 3:13–14).

²⁰ For all the promises of God find their Yes in him. That is why it is through him that we utter our Amen to God for his glory (2 Cor 1:20)

In the Church we see the superior glory of his power to redeem and sanctify a people for his name.

25 Husbands, love your wives, as Christ loved the church and gave himself up for her, 26 that he might sanctify her, having cleansed her by the washing of water with the word, 27 so that he might present the church to himself in splendor, without spot or wrinkle or any such thing, that she might be holy and without blemish. 28 In the same way husbands should love their wives as their own bodies. He who loves his wife loves himself (Eph 5:25–28).

1 Then I saw a new heaven and a new earth, for the first heaven and the first earth had passed away, and the sea was no more. 2 And I saw the holy city, new Jerusalem, coming down out of heaven from God, prepared as a bride adorned for her husband. 3 And I heard a loud voice from the throne saying, "Behold, the dwelling place of God is with man. He will dwell with them, and they will be his people, and God himself will be with them as their God (Rev 21:1–3).

Applying Biblical Themes

Teaching

BIBLICAL-THEOLOGICAL TEACHING is not set in contradistinction to expository preaching. Rather, expository preaching should evidence a commitment to Biblical Theology. Instead of teaching texts in isolation, expository preaching is done with regard to the greater framework of Biblical Theology. Whether teaching narrative or discourse, Scripture texts must always be related to the story line of the Bible. This does not diminish the value of exegeting texts within their immediate contexts, though it does encourage the interpreter to keep in view the entire scope of biblical-theology as the context for interpreting and applying Scripture. The proposed biblical-theological framework set forth in this paper offers the teacher a basis for always asking certain interpretive and application questions, such as these six biblical-theological questions to be asked in preparation for teaching:

1. How does this text relate to God's purposes through Christ in creation?

2. How does this text relate to the corruption of sin and Christ's victory over sin?

3. How does this text relate to God's covenant purposes in Christ?

4. How does this text relate to God's purposes in the cross of Christ?

5. How does this text relate to God's purposes through Christ in the church?

6. How does this text relate to God's purposes through Christ in the consummation?

We may also ask these six application questions in our preparation for preaching and teaching:

1. What does this text say about our responsibility to influence culture for Christ in carrying out our stewardship responsibilities?

2. What does this text say about the ramifications of depravity?

3. What does this text say about our responsibility to respond to the particular words of God in order to be faithful covenant keepers?

4. What does this text say about God's redemptive purposes in Christ?

5. What does this text say about my responsibilities and privileges as a member of "the people of God" under the Lordship of Christ?

6. What does this text say about life in relationship to Christ in the final consummation?

A Biblical Theme approach to presenting the gospel.

A biblical-theological approach will also influence how one presents the gospel. Actually, the presentation of the gospel becomes sort of an initial catechism, another means to reinforce the biblical-theological plot line. An example of a biblical-theological presentation of the gospel might be as follows:

A biblical-theological presentation of the Gospel [1]

---

1. Portions of this presentation are informed by *Two ways to Live* from Matthias Media.

1. God is the loving creator of the world.

   He created the world.

   He created us to be rulers of the world under Him. (Gen 1:1; John 1:1–3; Col 1:16–18).

2. But, we all have become corrupted, having rebelled in seeking to live life our own way

   Gen 3; Rom 3:10–12, Isa 53:6

3. God continually seeks out rebels through His Word (covenant) and calls them to a relationship with Himself.

   This relationship requires a response to His Word.

   Faith in God's Word is the single requirement. Faith implies obedience. Gen 3:9; Gen 12:1; 15:6; Eph 2:8–9

   Transition: The Ultimate call is through the cross of Jesus Christ.

4. God, through the cross of Christ, redeems those who have violated his Word (covenant breakers).

   I Pet 3:18; Gal 3:13;

5. God gathers those who believe His Word (covenant-keepers) into His church.

   Acts 2:41–42

6. God rewards the faithful (covenant keepers) and judges the unbelieving (covenant breakers) in the end.

   Matt 25:46; Rom 14:12; 2 Cor 10:5; Rev 20.

   Do you sense that God has been seeking you? Are you willing to believe that God has solved your sin problem through the death and resurrection of Jesus Christ? Today will you obey His Word by putting your faith in Jesus Christ and choosing to submit to Him?

The intent of presenting the gospel in a biblical-theological way is 1) to make clear the complicated scope of biblical revelation which we often assume, 2) to present a biblical message that is both content full and all-embracing, 3) to be able to converse with biblical illiterates by setting forth a biblical worldview.

Music in Corporate Worship

Hymn and chorus selections should be based not only on their theological accuracy and their stylistic beauty, but also on how they serve to develop and reinforce the story-line of Scripture. Service orders should be periodically examined as to the balance of biblical-theological teaching that is taking place. By using the chart presented on page 4, song selections can be charted on the story-line as well as according to the category of systematic theology.

Reading Clubs

For those who want to continue the study of Biblical Themes, the following texts can be utilized in reading clubs. A group of individuals might choose a book which they might choose to read over a designated period of time and then would meet together a number of times to discuss the issues in that book.

Reading for an Overview of Biblical Theology

Dentan, Robert. *The Design of the Scriptures. A First Reader in Biblical Theology.* New York: McGraw Hill, 1961.

Goldsworthy, Graeme. *According to Plan.* Leicester: InterVarsity, 1991.

———. *Gospel and Wisdom.* Carlisle, UK: Paternoster, 1987.

———. *Gospel in Revelation.* Carlisle, UK: Paternoster, 1984.

————. *Gospel and Kingdom.* Carlisle, UK: Paternoster, 1981.

Hasel, Gerhard. *Old Testament Theology: Basic Issues in the Current Debate.* Grand Rapids: Eerdmans, 1972.

Helyer, Larry R. *Yesterday, Today, and Forever.* Salem: Sheffield Publishing Co., 1996.

Jensen, Peter. *The Heart of the Universe.* Wheaton: Crossway, 1991.

Kerux. *A Journal of Biblical-Theological Preaching.* Escondido: Kerux, Inc.

Longman, Tremper, III. *Making Sense of the Old Testament.* Grand Rapids: Baker, 1998.

Vangemeren, Willem. *The Progress of Redemption.* Grand Rapids: Baker, 1988.

Vos, Geerhardus. *Biblical Theology. Old and New Testaments.* Edinburgh: Banner of Truth Trust, reprint 1996.

Biblical-theological Reading on Creation

Kline, Meredith G. *Images of the Spirit.* S. Hamilton, MA: Gordon-Conwell Theological Seminary, 1986.

————. *Kingdom Prologue.* S. Hamilton, MA: Gordon-Conwell Theological Seminary, 1989.

————. *Kingdom Prologue.* Vol.2. S. Hamilton, MA: Gordon-Conwell Theological Seminary, 1985.

Wolters, Albert. *Creation Regained. Biblical Basics for a Reformational Worldview.* Grand Rapids: Eerdmans, 1985.

Readings on Corruption

Plantinga, Cornelius, Jr. *Not the Way It's Supposed to Be.* Grand Rapids: Eerdmans, 1995.

Biblical-theological Reading on Covenants

Dumbrell, W. J. *Covenant and Creation. A Theology of Old Testament Covenants.* Nashville: Thomas Nelson, 1984.

Martens, Elmer A. *God's Design. A Focus on Old Testament Theology.* Grand Rapids: Baker, 1981.

McComiskey, Thomas Edward. *The Covenants of Promise. A Theology of Old Testament Covenants.* Grand Rapids: Baker, 1985.

Robertson, O. Palmer. *The Christ of the Covenants.* Phillipsburg: Presbyterian and Reformed, 1980.

Biblical-theological Reading on Christ and the Cross

Gaffin, Richard B. *Resurrection and Redemption. A Study in Paul's Soteriology.* Phillipsburg: Presbyterian and Reformed, 1978.

Green, Michael. *The Empty Cross of Jesus.* Downers Grove: InterVarsity, 1984.

Sauer, Erich. *The Triumph of the Crucified.* Grand Rapids: Eerdmans, 1972.

Stott, John R. W. The Cross of Christ. Downers Grove: InterVarsity, 1986.

Biblical-theological Reading on the Church

Mack, Wayne, and David Swavely. *Life in the Father's House.* Phillipsburg: Presbyterian and Reformed, 1996.

Dever, Mark. *Nine Marks of a Healthy Church.* Washington, DC: Center for Church Reform, 1998.

Vos, Geerhardus. *The Kingdom of God and the Church.* Nutley, NJ: Presbyterian and Reformed, 1972 reprint.

Biblical-theological Reading on the Consummation

Goldsworthy, Graeme. *Gospel in Revelation.* Carlisle, UK: Paternoster, 1994.

Hoekma, A. A. *The Bible and the Future.* Grand Rapids: Eerdmans, 1979.

Ladd, G. E. *The Blessed Hope.* Grand Rapids: Eerdmans, 1956.

Ryrie, Charles. *The Basis of the Premillennial Faith.* Neptune: Loizeaux, 1953.

Waldron, Samuel E. *The End Times Made Simple.* Amityville: Calvary, 2003.

Reading in Apologetics

Frame, John. *Apologetics to the Glory of God*. Phillipsburg: Presbyterian and Reformed, 1994.

Reading in Hermeneutics

McCartney, Dan, and Charles Clayton. *Let the Reader Understand*. Wheaton: Victor Books, 1994.

Vanhoozer, Kevin J. *Is there a Meaning in this Text?* Grand Rapids: Zondervan, 1998.

Zuck, Roy B., ed. *Rightly Divided*. Grand Rapids: Kregel, 1996.

Reading in Postmodernism

Carson, D. A. *The Gagging of God*. Grand Rapids: Zondervan, 1996.

Erickson, Millard. *Postmodernizing the Faith*. Grand Rapids: Baker, 1998.

Bibliography

Andrews, Robert G. "Romans 11:11–32. The Future of Israel." *Th.M. Thesis.* Westminster Theological Seminary, 1982.

Arndt, W. F. and Gingrich, F. W. *A Greek – English Lexicon of the New Testament and Other Early Christian Literature.* Chicago: University of Chicago, 1957.

Carson, D. A. "Current Issues in Biblical Theology." *Bulletin for Biblical Research* 5 (1995) 17–41.

————. *The Gagging of God.* Grand Rapids: Zondervan, 1996.

————. "Unity and Diversity in the N.T.: The Possibility of Systematic Theology." In *Scripture and Truth*, edited by D. A. Carson and J. D. Woodbridge, 65–95. Zondervan, 1983.

Childs, Brevard. *Biblical Theology in Crisis.* Louisville: Westminster, 1970.

————. *The Christology of the New Testament.* London: SCM, 1967.

Biblical Theology of the Old and New Testaments. Minneapolis: Fortress, 1992.

Clines, David J. A. *The Theme of the Pentateuch.* Sheffield: Sheffield, 1997.

Cullman, Oscar. *Christ and Time.* Louisville: Westminster, 1975.

————. *The Christology of the New Testament.* London: SCM, 1967.

Culver, Robert D. *Toward a Biblical View of Civil Government.* Chicago: Moody, 1974.

Daniels, Dwight R., and Bernd Janowski. "Literatur zur Biblischen Theologie 19851988." *JBTh* 4 (1989) 301–47.

Dentan, Robert. *The Design of the Scriptures. A First Reader in Biblical Theology.* New York: McGraw Hill, 1961.

Dever, Mark. *Nine Marks of a Healthy Church.* Washington, D.C.: Center for Church Reform, 1998.

Dumbrell, William J. *Covenant and Creation.* Nashville: Nelson, 1984.

Erickson, Millard. *Postmodernizing the Faith.* Grand Rapids: Baker, 1998.

Feinberg, John S., and Paul D. Feinberg, eds. *Tradition and Testament. Essays in Honor of Charles Lee Feinberg.* Chicago: Moody, 1981.

Frame, John. *Apologetics to the Glory of God.* Phillipsburg: Presbyterian and Reformed Publishing, 1994.

Fuller, Daniel P. *Gospel & Law. Contrast or Continuum. The Hermeneutics of Dispensationalism and Covenant Theology.* Grand Rapids: Eerdmans, 1980.

―――. "The Hermeneutics of Dispensationalism." Doctoral Dissertation, Northern Baptist Theological Seminary, 1957.

―――. *The Unity of the Bible.* Grand Rapids: Zondervan, 1992.

Gaffin, Richard B. *Resurrection and Redemption. A Study in Paul's Soteriology.* Phillipsburg: Presbyterian and Reformed, 1978.

Goldsworthy, Graeme. *According to Plan.* Leicester, England: InterVarsity, 1991.

Green, Michael. *The Empty Cross of Jesus.* Downers Grove: InterVarsity, 1984.

Hasel, G.F. "Biblical Theology: Then, Now, and Tomorrow." *Horizons in Biblical Theology* 4 (1982) 6193.

―――. *Old Testament Theology: Basic Issues in the Current Debate.* Grand Rapids: Eerdmans, 1991.

―――. "The Relationship between Biblical Theology and Systematic Theology." *TrinJ* 5 (1984) 113-27.

Helyer, Larry R. *Yesterday, Today, and Forever.* Salem: Sheffield Publishing Co., 1996.

Hengstenberg, E. W. *Christology of the Old Testament.* Grand Rapids: Kregel, 1970.

Hoekma, A. A. *The Bible and the Future.* Grand Rapids: Eerdmans, 1979.

Jensen, Peter. *The Heart of the Universe.* Wheaton: Crossway, 1991.

Kaiser, Walter C., Jr. *Toward and Old Testament Theology.* Grand Rapids: Zondervan, 1978.

―――. *The Uses of the Old Testament in the New.* Chicago: Moody Press, 1985.

Kline, Meredith. *Images of the Spirit.* Grand Rapids: Baker, 1980.

―――. *Kingdom Prologue.* 3 vols, GordonConwell: unpublished syllabus.

Ladd, G. E. *The Blessed Hope.* Grand Rapids: Eerdmans, 1956.

Longman, Tremper, III. *Making Sense of the Old Testament.* Grand Rapids: Baker, 1998.

Lillback, Peter Alan. *The Binding of God. Calvin's Role in the Development of Covenant Theology.* Ph.D. Dissertation. Westminster Theological Seminary, 1985.

Mack, Wayne, and David Swavely. *Life in the Father's House.* Phillipsburg: Presbyterian and Reformed Publishing, 1996.

Martens, Elmer A. *God's Design. A Focus on Old Testament Theology.* Grand Rapids: Baker, 1981.

McComiskey, Thomas Edward. *The Covenants of Promise. A Theology of Old Testament Covenants.* Grand Rapids: Baker, 1985.

Peters, G. N. H. *The Theocratic Kingdom.* Vol. 1. Grand Rapids: Baker, 1970.

Poythress, Vern. *The Shadow of Christ in the Law of Moses.* Brentwood: Wolgemuth & Hyatt, 1991.

Richardson, Alan. *Theological Wordbook of the Bible.* New York: Macmillan, 1950.

Robertson, O. Palmer. *The Christ of the Covenants*. Phillipsburg: Presbyterian and Reformed, 1980.

———. "Genesis 15:6; New Covenant Expositions of an Old Covenant Text." *WTJ* 42 (1980) 259–89.

Ryrie, Charles. *The Basis of the Premillennial Faith*. Neptune: Loizeaux, 1953.

Sauer, Erich. *The Triumph of the Crucified*. Grand Rapids: Eerdmans, 1972.

Stott, John R. W. *The Cross of Christ*. Downers Grove: InterVarsity, 1986.

Two Ways to Live. Youngstown: Matthias Media, 2021.

VanGemeren, Willem. *The Progress of Redemption*. Grand Rapids: Zondervan, 1988.

Vanhoozer, Kevin J. *Is there a Meaning in this Text?* Grand Rapids: Zondervan, 1998.

Vos, Geerhardus. *Biblical Theology. Old and New Testaments*. Grand Rapids: Eerdmans, 1985.

———. *The Kingdom of God and the Church*. Phillipsburg: Presbyterian and Reformed, 1972.

Waltke, Bruce. "Old Testament Biblical Theology." Class notes. Westminster Theological Seminary, 1986.

Walton, John H. *Covenant. God's Purpose. God's Plan*. Grand Rapids: Zondervan, 1994.

Wolters, Albert. *Creation Regained. Biblical Basics for a Reformational Worldview*. Grand Rapids: Eerdmans, 1985.

Wouldstra, Martin. "Israel and the Church: A Case for Continuity." In *Continuity and Discontinuity*, edited by John Feinberg, 221–38. Westchester: Crossway, 1988.

9 781666 737394